HOW TO BE THE BEST MANAGER ON THE PLANET

HOW TO BE THE BEST MANAGER

ON THE PLANET

▼

The 6 simple rules to becoming

a Top notch manager of people

John Gaddis

Writers Club Press

San Jose New York Lincoln Shanghai

How to be the Best Manager on the Planet
The 6 simple rules to becoming a Top notch manager of people

Writers Club Press
an imprint of iUniverse.com, Inc.

For information address:
iUniverse.com, Inc.
5220 S 16th, Ste. 200
Lincoln, NE 68512
www.iuniverse.com

ISBN: 0-595-19657-8

Printed in the United States of America

CONTENTS

▼

Don't just think your good,
Be able to back it up!

FOREWORD

▼

The purpose of this book is simple. It is to give you all the information and tools you need to become the very best manager on this planet. It will allow you to become a manager far and above anything you have ever seen or done before. And if you choose to do this, it will literally change your life and the lives of the people around you.

The problem you face as a manager is also simple. Nobody has taught you how to do the job of management. Up till now you have only been shown just bits and pieces of your job as a manager. Perhaps you were sent to a class or maybe you even bought a book or two on the subject. But nobody ever sat down with you and told you how to manage people from the A to Z. Nobody has ever told you how important your job really is. Nor did they tell you what to look for to know that you are doing your job properly. They didn't tell you how many people you can affect on any given day that you go to work. They didn't tell you these things for a reason, because they didn't know themselves. Because nobody had ever taught them. So how could they possibly teach you anything about management?

Well, that is about to change. In this book you are going to find all the basics you need to know to become the very best manager on the planet. You know that old saying" *Build your castle in the sky, but build your foundation on solid rock* ". That's what this information in this book will do for you. It will give you a rock solid foundation on which to build your castle in the sky. Everything in this book is tried and true. It works because it has a track record of working. These are fundamental laws that have proven themselves throughout time.

Some the things in this book you have heard before. Some other things you have never heard quite like this. Everything that I talk about it simple and easy to do. There is nothing difficult about any of this. You only have to do one thing. And that is to *just do it.* If you do these things on a daily basis, over and over again, you will notice a subtle but monumental change occurring not only in your job but in your life.

Your job is a manager is one of the most important jobs on this planet, if not *the* most important one. Especially in this day and age. We have never needed managers who are good at their job, than we do today. We need high quality managers more than anything else today. We need people who can step up and get the job done the way it is supposed to be done, rather than the way it has been done. Unfortunately, as a manager today you have been shown a lot of things that do not work. And by accepting those as the accepted way of doing business you have been paying a very serious price that you are not aware of. Throughout this book we will be looking at a lot of different ways of doing your job so that you no longer have to pay that price. And unfortunately since you are a manager, any price that you pay for doing the job wrong, is also paid for by the people that depend on you. Namely all the people that you manage. So the other thing that you are going to learn about is just how much it costs to do things the old way. And when you find out how expensive it is you might want to rethink your position on doing those ways. I certainly hope so. And so do a lot of other people who depend on you.

Everything that you are going to read about is a tried and true tested way of taking care of business. And what you are about to become should you choose to do these things, is a very super-efficient manager of people. Everything about your job is about to change. How you look at your life, how you look at the people you work with and how you look at your job, are about to undergo a radical change. And everything is going to be for the better. I guarantee it.

In this book you are going to learn the six things you need to know to be the best manager on this planet. They will form your foundation for which to go out and perform your duties as a manager every single day. You do the six things on a daily basis, even a little at time and everything will begin to change for the better for you. Nobody but nobody will be able to beat you at managing people. There is winning and there is losing. This is about winning. I am not going to pull any of my punches for you. I am going to be upfront and brutally honest about everything I tell you. I repeat, I am going to be brutally honest with you. This is the best way to get at our problems and solutions. This is about being the best manager on the planet, period.

Each other six things that it takes to be the best manager on this planet are going to be your foundation. If I was going to build a foundation out of six separate pieces, I would not have a foundation as strong as a single piece. That is the beauty of the six ideas. All six of them are linked together. You cannot have one without the other. All six pieces interconnect. So when you put all six pieces together, you end up with a single piece foundation. That is the strongest foundation that you can have. So if you try to do just one of the ideas you will find that you also have to do the others. If I wanted to build a foundation for my house for instance, a solid single piece foundation would be much stronger than six separate pieces. So you will soon see that every idea in this book is linked to every other idea in the book. This will end up creating the best possible foundation for you. This book is not intended to be an end all and be all to management. Your job as a manager is an ongoing learning process. There are all kinds of other things that you can study to help you do your job better. You can study human psychology. You can study body language. You can study just about anything that involves human beings. This book is intended to give you a rock solid foundation to be the best manager on this planet. And if you do nothing more than just what I talk about in this book, you will still end up being one of the best managers on this planet, period. By studying other things you just become better at it. Plus, it is always good to keep the learning process going. You actually can learn something new every day, no matter how good you are.

As you read about the different subject's in this book, I want you to read them with an open mind. Do not write anything off as being silly or overly simplistic. I could have written a very large book for you to read, but what would have happened is that you would have read it once, put it on your shelf and there it would have stayed. This book is intended to be something that you can reference anytime you like or inexpensive enough that you can give it to a friend.

I am sure that you have watched children learning something new. They always seem to learn something new very quickly. Do you know why this is? It is because children do not think so much about what they are learning. When we become adults, when we try something new we tend to think too much. For some reason as adults we want to make things much more difficult than they really are. The trick to learning something new is to stop thinking so much. Do not make it more difficult than it has to be. There are a lot of people who think that managing people is a difficult task. It is usually a difficult task for them for two simple reasons. One is, they think too much. Secondly, they are most likely doing it the hard way. So, as you read this book just relax and think about what you read in the simplest manner that you can. Nobody is holding a gun to your head to do any of this. Relax. If you do not like what you read, you can just toss the book into the garbage. But if you do like what you read, you had better watch out. You just might end up being the best manager on the planet. No risk, possible large payoff. What could be better than that? Remember, keep it simple. And best of all, have fun!

But, before we get started let me ask you a simple question. What if tomorrow you went to work and someone else was controlling the future of your employment as a manager? No longer was your boss the one in charge of your employment. What if the people that you manage had a say in your future? Just for fun let's give them all a vote. This vote will be totally secret. A simple yes or no as whether to keep you in charge or not. A simple majority either way. Do you think that you would be able to keep your job? You would be surprised at how many managers would not survive the vote. Let's make absolutely certain that you would. Everything that you need will be presented to you in this book.

CHAPTER 1

▼

FIRST THINGS FIRST

Before we can get started on the six things that make up your foundation as a manager, we must make some changes first. And there are also a few rules of the road that you need to know that affect your job. There are certain rules, just like driving a car that you need to know to be able to do your job properly. Unfortunately nobody has made you aware of them. So we will discuss them in this chapter so you can get a better understanding of what you need to do to become the best manager on this planet.

NEW NAME

First of all we've got to change your title. Perhaps you are called a manager or a supervisor or some other title. Unfortunately none of those titles actually reflect what your job really is. If I were to ask you right now to write down in one sentence exactly what your job really is, could you do it? Include everything in it in one single sentence? How about this? It is to bring out the best in your people and yourself for the benefit of not only of the company and your customers but you and your employees. If you would do that no matter what business you were in, you would be an extremely successful person. And your company would be a very successful company. It mattered not what you were doing as a company. And nothing describes what your job is more than a single word.... Leader. You are a Leader! And by seeing that you are a leader you have set in motion certain rules now that allow you to play at a much higher level. The word leader is an active noun. It not only states your job title, but it also states what you do in your job. You lead people. If you want higher morale in your company, then you lead people to higher morale. If you want better communications in your company, then you lead people to better communications. If you want better teamwork, then you lead people to better teamwork. In this simple line of thinking about your job you can begin to see already why certain workplaces have done poorly at managing their people and have failed to function properly as a team. Just by understanding the fact that you lead people changes the way you look at your job. How many managers in your past work history could you consider to be truly a leader? I doubt that there was an abundance of them. And there in that simple definition lies the problem. People just do not look at themselves as leaders. They are merely managers or supervisors of people. If you wanted to get a project done would you choose a manager, a supervisor or would you choose a leader? Just by redefining your job title, you set in motion all sorts of new ways in dealing with your work environment. If you did nothing more than just change your name in your mind to leader and understood that simple fact without doing anything else in this book, you would be twice the manager that you are now. So from now on, you are to see yourself only as a leader. This is your first step in becoming the best manager on the planet.

FEAR AND DESIRE

To be a really good manager you have to understand some things about people. It is after all people that you are going to manage. The more that you understand about your people of, the better able you are to do your job.

Let's say that you want to learn to hunt. Before you can become a good hunter, you must understand your quarry. The more you know about your quarry's habits and movements, the better chance you have at hunting. If you knew nothing at all about your quarry and went into the woods to hunt you would most likely be very unsuccessful. You might get lucky once in awhile, but in the long run you would do poorly as a hunter. If you knew your quarry's habits and movements and how they interacted with their environment, you would be able to seek out situations that increase your chances of being successful. The more you understood your quarry, the more successful you would be. This is a lot like management. The more you understand your people, their habits, their desires and their needs, the more successful you will be as a manager. You must have an understanding of human beings to be successful as a manager. The more you know about human beings and their habits and desires, the more successful you'll be leading these people. It is also to your advantage that you understand yourself. The more you understand how you react in certain situations, what you want from life and the things that drive you in your life, the more successful you will be. Let's say that you're a person who cannot take criticism very well. For some reason in your life you are just not able to tolerate people criticizing your behavior. I have run across a lot of people like this in my life. The people on the surface appear to be very confident and knowledgeable about their job. But if anybody criticizes them about their work, they would not be able to handle that criticism very well. What this works out to be is a weakness on the part of that manager. Since the manager did not understand that he had this weakness, he was not able to deal with it very well. In fact, the chances were that he would never deal with it. A simple lack of understanding on his part about himself in that situation would pose a problem to him and everybody that would have to depend on him during their working life. To remedy that situation you need to be able to sit down and take a hard look at yourself, your actions and how you handle yourself in any given situation. You must be brutal in your assessment of who you are and how you would react. Most people do not want to do that with themselves. They would rather avoid that at all costs. To be a successful human being or the best manager of the planet you must be able to look at all your strengths and weaknesses in the harsh light of day. You absolutely have to do this. The more you're able to do that, the more weaknesses and strengths you'll find and therefore be able to deal with them so much better. There is nothing wrong with having weaknesses. Everybody has them. But if you want to be successful you must look at your weaknesses and either fined a way to get rid yourself of them or at the very least find a way to deal with them so they are not problematic in your work or personal life.

This book is not intended to be an end all and be all of management. If you do things that I talk about in this book, you'll still be the best manager on the planet. Period. However you can go farther and farther with this if you choose to. By taking a course in human behavior or human interaction, etc. the more you can increase your chances of being successful as a manager. The more that you understand about people and yourself, the better manager you will become. Become a student of not only people, but yourself as well.

This section is dedicated to the basic fear and desire of any human being. What you want to know is the basic fear and desire of any human being. Go right to the source. Cut to the chase. Find out what the bottom line is with any human being. By cutting to the chase and getting to the core of the problem, you have a much greater chance of solving that problem than someone who merely moves around on the edges of a problem. To paraphrase Henry David Thoreau, "many hack at the branches of a problem, but few hack at the roots". If you really want to solve anything or understand anything, you must go to the very core level of the situation to understand and to solve that situation. If you merely move around on the edges and like so many people do, you'll have a very hard time understanding and solving the situation.

Do you know what the greatest desire of all people is? It is to be accepted. Do you know what the greatest fear of all people is? It is to be rejected. So if you understand these two desires, it brings about a certain understanding of the people you manage. If I understand that the greatest desire is to be accepted, then if I create a situation that makes people feel the most accepted, and then I will have created a situation which brings out the best in people. And conversely, if I understand that their greatest fear is rejection, then if I am a good manager I will try to avoid anything that makes my people feel rejected. Almost everyone wants to be part of a team. They want to be part of a team because it makes them feel wanted and accepted. No one wants to come to work and feel like they are an outsider. You know from your own work experience that you feel most comfortable when everybody's accepting each other and working together for the common goal. However, some of your most uncomfortable days at work were usually when there was tension among the team and the common goal was not in sight that day. So it is paramount in your job as a leader to make sure that everybody feels accepted and comfortable in the team. Anything that makes a team member feel left out of the team is going to be an unnecessary problem that gets in the way of your goal. Do not let dissension enter in your team. And if you see the beginnings of dissension seeping in, stop and immediately take care of it and remove it from the team. How do you take care of dissention? You sit down with individuals or the team, and you find out exactly what the problem is. Once you find out what the problem is, you can begin to find solutions that will solve the problem. Do not ever dictate a solution to the problem. It is much simpler to solve a problem in its infancy, than to wait until it becomes a full-blown problem that causes other problems among your team. A good leader is always on the lookout for any problem that is going to hinder the functioning of the team. Always stay vigilant. It is the easiest and simplest way to control your problems. Why put up with problems when you do not have to?

As with everything else that we deal with, it is imperative that you make your people feel accepted into the team. Even when the team becomes very smooth in its operation, you must continually do a reality check to make sure that rejection is not seeping into the team. It is much easier to do this when you are ahead of the curve. Solve the problem of acceptance as best you can, and then do all you can to keep it moving. Do not go stagnant on yourself or the team. Continually be on the lookout for anything that may seep into the team that can cause the team problems.

ELEVATION BY DEGRADATION

Of all the things that you are going to learn about, your ego is the most insidious of them all. Bringing your ego to work is one of the most disruptive things that you can do in your job as a leader. Your ego represents you as an individual. It means me. When you are a leader of a group of people, there is only We. It may sound facetious to say it, but there is no room for I in we. In all my years in the workplace the most damaging of all single things that managers do, is to bring their ego to work. Check your ego at the door. Your ego represents me as the individual not the group. In management we are talking about a group of people, not the individual. When you are off the job, you are free to pursue your ego in any way, shape or form that you want. However, when you step into a team environment you must not bring your ego in to that environment. You're egos' only goal is to only think of you. That is not the case in a team. You must be thinking of what it takes to make the team better. Bringing your ego into the team does not make the team better. It goes against the very definition of what your job as a leader is. Unless of course, you have a particular desire to lose. You don't have that desire, do you?

Now there are probably plenty of people that would disagree with the statement that their ego is a hindrance to the team. However, I guarantee you that if they check their ego at the door; they would be seeing far better results than they are now. Since they are not doing that, does not mean for a second that if you bring your ego to work it is a positive thing. It only means that they have not tried a better way.

So what is elevation by degradation? It is what appears to be the simplest way to make myself feel that I am superior to you. All that I have to do is to *think* in my mind that I am better than you, and then I can have a superior feeling about myself compared to you. I do not have to do any of the work to make myself better. All I have to do is merely think that I am better than you. Unfortunately, this is a very commonplace line of thinking on this planet. You see it everywhere. White people thinking they are superior to black people. Men feeling superior to women. Rich people better than poor people. It's everywhere. And it is a very damaging line of thinking. It does not produce results necessary to win. It is self-defeating behavior. Nobody, but nobody, is better than anybody else, period. And when I say that it only appears to be the simplest way that is what I mean. It only appears that way. In actuality, it is the most difficult road of all to think that you are superior to anyone else. Too many problems come from this line of thinking. How can we all work as a team, when we see each other as a separate group from each other group? Think about this for a minute. What if you went to work tomorrow and every group in your company worked smoothly with every other group? Management and employees were on the same page. Customer service and production worked hand in hand. Don't you think that things would be a lot better? Thinking that you are the same as everyone else and they are just as important as you as well as anybody else produces much better results when trying to solve our problems. The "I'm better than you are" thinking is basically a complete failure. It only creates an illusion in your mind that is not true in reality. If it is not true in reality, it is of very little value to your company. You want to be the best manager on the planet. You have no time for illusions.

How many times have you been around a person who thought they were the greatest thing since the invention of the wheel? I'm sure that in your years of working you have been around more than one of these people. Did these people make you feel comfortable? Did anyone of them make you feel that they could do what they say they can do? Were these people a positive or a negative influence on your company? Chances are, that they were actually detrimental to the team and the company. People do not like to be around other people that think they are better than everyone else. There was even a car commercial recently that made the statement that buying their car would give you the feeling of "*I'm better than you are*". This kind of thinking does not bring out the best in anyone. Neither the individual nor the team. That goes for the CEO down to the mailroom clerk. If you want to think that you are special, and really be able to back it up, then be a serious team player. There are not many managers that can do that. *A group of people working together can do absolutely anything.* An individual working alone rarely can do that. By bringing individual thinking that says "I'm better than you" are into a team environment is extremely detrimental to that team. Again, it is something that you must stay vigilant for and remove as soon as you see it. It may be funny at first, but as it grows it will become very detrimental to your team.

A person that thinks that they are better than others creates serious problems for themselves and the team. This individual is going to have serious problems in being able to take a hard reality check of the way they do their job. They are continually making the assumption that they know what they are doing. Some will think that because they have a certain job that they must be better than the people "below them". It is quite possible that you can go through life and have all the trappings of success, and still be a failure as a manager, simply because you choose not to take a hard look at the way you do your job. Thinking you are better than someone else automatically put blinders around your perception of a situation. By putting those blinders on your perception you have effectively limited your ability to understand and do your job is a manager properly.

Let's say for instance that you are a man who believes that men are more important than women. This is a very common assumption. And it can be shown in the fact that women only make 76 percent of what men do doing the same job. You can see it in the fact that very few women are able to make it through the glass ceiling into the upper echelons of management. Now let's put this man in charge of a group of women in an office. Every time that this man has to deal with an individual or the team and he allows his perception that he is better than women to color his vision, he is going to let his assumptions continually block out his ability to actually see the problems and the solutions as they really are. His assumptions put blinders on his ability to logically look at a situation and understand it fully. Since this man allows his assumptions to interfere with his ability to understand the situation, his solution is going to be tainted at the very least. Most likely he will not only not solve the problem, but he will compound it and makes it worse. There are a lot of men in this world that assume that women should be subservient to men. Since they do not wish to see that everyone in the team is equal, instead of solving problems they cause more problems. And by the way, one of the best managers I have been around was a woman. By not looking at everyone as equal and not being able to sit down and look at a situation or a problem logically, you are going to have very poor results at best. Is this what you want? Is this what you think makes you a better manager? Does this make you a better human being? Like I said in the beginning of this book I was going to be brutally honest with you. And I want you to be brutally honest with yourself. If there are lines of thinking that you use that do not work or they perform poorly, you must get rid of them. It is much easier to rid yourself of these lines of thinking that it is to continue using them. You will be in effect doing things the hard way. And you'll have no one to blame but yourself. Is doing your job the hard way a choice that you wish to make?

So as to let you know that I am not picking on others, I am going to pick on myself here and show you that I to have done that. When we were younger our country called on us to go to war. When we came home from the war, the reception that we got was terrible to say the least. We had all put our lives on the line for our country when it had called, and when we came home we were spit upon and called all sorts of terrible things. (Just a little sidebar here, but if you really want to hurt someone, shun them. That plays on the fear of rejection quite well). We were accused of killing babies by sticking them with our bayonets among other things. Now, that is quite an awful thing to say about someone. That we would not only killed babies, but we would kill them with a bayonet. What kind of monsters would do something like that? And since they were accusing us of doing that, then *we* were the monsters. People said that it was OK for our wives to be sleeping around while we were off to war. In short, they treated us about as bad as you could treat another human being. So what did I do? After I got over the shock of the homecoming, I stepped into my own little world of elevation by degradation. I figured that since I had lived through something so awful, something that they do not wish to understand, then I was better than they were. Since all I wanted was just a little respect for having gone through this war, I proceeded to find myself an outlet where I thought I could earn some respect. I found that outlet in my job. What I did for a living to earn money. I figured that if I did my job better than anybody else did, then I would surely earn myself some respect. And that's what I did. I went to work each day with a single thought in mind. Come hell or high water, I was going to beat everybody at what I did. And I became very good what I did. However, I was not somebody that you would like to have been around. What I finally learned was, that it wasn't the respect of others that I was seeking, it was the respect of myself that I was seeking. I had tried to make myself better than others. And all that I did was to increase the loss that I already had. Once I dropped that line of thinking, things became a lot better for me. Now, instead of seeking the respect of others, I seek only to respect myself. And by doing so, I take care of everything else in the process. Once I stopped thinking that I was better than anybody else, and started seeing myself as part of a team, everything in my life began to turn for the better. So when I talk about elevation by degradation, I know a little bit about what I am talking about.

YARDSTICK

So how are you going to know that what you're doing as a manager is really true? What do you use as a measurement to judge what is actually going on with your management techniques? And then you are going to need some kind of a guide to let you know if you are on track or not. There are two basic ways of assessing a situation. There is what you *think* has happened and there is what has *actually* happened. Sometimes they converge, sometimes they don't. So how are we going to separate the two?

If you use the first way of assessing a situation, you will be using the worst of all. That is using your personal opinion to judge what is going on. The problem with a personal opinion is this that they are sometimes right and they are sometimes wrong. So if I was going to measure something would I use a measuring stick that was sometimes right and sometimes wrong? You can imagine that if I used that to build a house, I would certainly run into serious problems in a hurry. You can believe that God is a three legged chicken; however that doesn't necessarily mean He is. All that means is, that is what you think. Personal opinions about what you are doing and the actual truth of what you are doing have a correlation in science. In science there are theories and there are laws. A theory may turn into a law but that does not mean that all theories will become laws. Science uses laws to explain the universe. If a scientist used a theory to explain the universe, we would certainly run into some serious problems. We might believe that the earth is flat, or that the sun revolves around the earth. Let me give you an example of what I am talking about. Let's say that we want to put a man on the moon. We do not understand the laws of the solar system, yet we have lots of opinions on how we *think* it works. Here's the scene: we have three astronauts sitting down getting their final briefing from the head scientist of the moon launch. And the astronauts are in full gear ready to board the spaceship that will take them into space. The scientist begins the by telling them how he thinks the mission will go. The scientist points up at the moon and then glances over at the spaceship and then looks at the astronauts. He picks up a blade of grass to test the wind and begins to tell the astronauts that if they launch fairly quickly, with the moon in its present position that they might be able to hit it dead on. That is of course, if the wind stays at its present direction. He tells them that he *thinks* they have a good chance of making it. You can guess what the scene looks like now. You have three astronauts in full space gear running as fast as they can away from that launch pad. And there in lies the problem with personal opinions. Sometimes they are right and sometimes they are wrong. I am not saying there is anything wrong with personal opinions per se, I'm just saying be very careful when you have to deal with them. Check them out before you use them, and you will save yourself a lot of trouble.

Just like those astronauts, I do not feel comfortable risking what I do on a line of thinking that may or may not be true. If I'm going to put it on the line, so to speak, I want to know upfront that what I am going to use flat out gets it done. Why take a gamble when you do not have to? Wouldn't you rather use a line of thinking that you knew upfront worked and had a track record of working, rather than gamble on a personal opinion that may or may not be true? How many managers had you noticed that did things in the workplace that you knew for a fact was inefficient or just downright damaging? I'll bet that you have known more than a few. And that is simply because those managers never bothered to check out their line of thinking. They went with a personal opinion when they should have gone with a line of thinking that had a track record of winning consistently. If you hear someone start a sentence with the words "I think" or "We think" a red flag should go up in your mind. What that person is about to give you is a personal opinion. That is all well and good by itself. But remember it is just a personal opinion. How many times have you heard a manager say I think so and so is doing a great job? When in reality you knew that so and so was basically nothing more than a yes man. The manager may think that so and so is doing a good job but in reality the other members of the team would never count on so and so to handle their portion of the job properly.

So, what do you do now? Like everything else the answer is simple and straightforward. All the information that you need to do your job and become the best manager on this planet is available to you right now. The problems of communication, teamwork, respect, problem solving and leadership have all been answered. They have all been done before. It is just a matter of using the same information that the people who had done it before have used. The things that I am telling you about in this book are not my own. I did not think of them. I can make no claim on them at all. All I have done is put them in a package for you. That is it. The problems that you face as a manager have all been solved before. Now just use the information about all that's been done about those problems for your own benefit. There is no reason to continue going through the same old problems day in and day out at work, when all the solutions are available to you and every other manager that exists on the face of this earth. It has all been done before. There are only two reasons why anyone would not use this proven information to do their job. First, they did not know about the information or they did not know where to find it. The information in this book will put you well on your way to acquiring the information that you need to be the best manager on this planet. The second reason is, they have a personal problem. Elevation by degradation is a prime example.

Another good alternative to checking whether your line of thinking works is to find a disinterested third party. Sometimes these people are called a personal coach. Perhaps it is a good friend whose viewpoint is one that you can trust. But they are usually somebody who you trust but have no interest in the outcome of the situation. That is, their thinking is not tainted by which ever direction you should choose. These people can be of great help to you if you seek them out. I highly recommend this way of looking at things. In fact, find more than one if you can. Second and third viewpoints are even better. They make doing a reality check so much easier. And it is just another way to back up your thinking to make sure it works. It is cheaper and easier to check your line of thinking every now and then, no matter how successful you are. You can subtly get sidetracked without knowing it. A disinterested third person will help to keep you on track. It is just smart thinking. You still like winning, don't you?

LIKE ATTRACTS LIKE

Another rule that you need to be aware of it is that like attracts like. What that means is that people tend to want to be around people like themselves who share a common interest. If I like golf, then I will like to be around people that like to golf. People like to be around other people that share their common interest. It just makes them feel comfortable. It is a something that people naturally do. But the problem to you as a manager is this. Did you ever wonder why certain people got promoted and others did not? Why one person who seemed a much better fit for a management promotion and would not get promoted, when a person that did not seem right for the job would get promoted? Generally what is happening is the manager of them is merely promoting someone because they feel more comfortable with that person. So, if you have a manager that is not very good at what he does, he was going to promote someone who has a similar philosophy as his own, someone who is also not very good at what they do. Why would he want to promote someone that would make him look like he was not doing his job properly? That would be self-defeating on his part. So people generally do not promote the best and the brightest. They like to talk about it a lot, but they rarely do it.

Let me tell you about a company that I know about that had a yes man running one of their plants. Since this manager was allowed to be in charge of this plant for a lengthy period of time, what happened was every time an opening came up for a manager, the person promoted was a yes man also. Like attracts like. And since managers tend to promote people like themselves, then given enough time all the management positions will be filled with people very similar to the Boss. Unfortunately, if you have a manager of an office or a plant or a company who's not very good at managing people, then they will tend to bring more and more people into the management fold that also do not know how to manage people. It is just a natural thing that people do. Like that old saying "one bad apple spoils the whole box" you can quickly see that one bad manager at the top of a plant or a company can also be detrimental to the plant or company. I'm sure that in your working experiences you have noticed places that acted very similar to this. That the managers tend to be pretty much alike. That is why it is imperative to promote and train good people to be managers in your company. You must always strive to choose the best and the brightest to bring up through the ranks. A good test to give any of your managers is to poll the team. Let the people say anything that they want in complete secrecy. Without fear of retribution your people will tell you pretty much the truth. It is pretty simple to get the information you need to be the best manager on the planet. Again constant vigilance on your part will keep this problem to an absolute minimum. It is much easier to solve a problem in its infancy, than to let it grow and fester and become a large problem. Constant vigilance on your part is actually a very simple thing to do. If you know what you are looking for, then it is easy to keep an eye out for it.

STRESS

Now let's talk a little about stress. There are some normal stresses that occur in the workplace. Maybe you have an assignment that is due at a certain time, or when everybody is working to get a new product out on a certain date. A certain amount of stress just naturally occurs in the workplace. That is not the kind of stress that I am talking about. I am talking about the other stress—the unnecessary stress. I am talking about the unnecessary stress of office politics, infighting, favoritism, not listening to employees concerns, and so on and so on. This is the kind of stress need not be in the workplace. This stress is *toxic*. To much stress on a person is a toxin. There are many medical studies on this very subject that prove the point over and over. This is something you should avoid at all costs. When people are put under undo stress, what you end up with is people becoming sick, taking extra leave days, and basically impacting your health costs. Controlling undue stress in the workplace is one of the single biggest things you can do to control your health costs. If people come to work every single day and face too much stress you are not only going to have inefficient employees but your going to have more sick employees. And undue stress kept up over a long period of time will cause serious health problems for your people.

I knew of a company that had a running joke about who could retire without having bypass surgery. Now this may sound funny but the reality was that approximately two-thirds of those who had retired had had bypass surgery before their retirement. Now a certain argument can be made about the American diet. I think that if you run the numbers you'll find that two-thirds is certainly on the high side. The company's biggest problem was this low-level stress that occurred on a daily basis. People knew that every day was going to be the same as the last day. Sort of like Groundhog Day. Nothing was going to change; nothing was going to get any better. There would be no progress, only stagnation. When your people start thinking like this, you are going to have all kinds of problems. But what we're talking about here in this section is stress. The kind of stress that comes with poor communication, lack of teamwork, very little if any leadership, and certainly no passion about coming to work. Is this how you would want your work days to be like?

You wouldn't knowingly walk in asbestos and then walk into your home. That would be totally foolish. You would never want to bring a toxin like asbestos into your family home. And yet managers and companies will allow this undue stress to come to the workplace just like asbestos fibers, and not think twice about it. It makes no sense and all. When health costs are the single most explosive expense for companies right now, why would anybody want to add to them unnecessarily? Stress is toxic to your people and your company. You must always strive to reduce this stress. It brings you and the company no good whatsoever and it cost you in the short run and the long run. It is just a plain expensive and foolish way to run a business. All down side and no upside. A fool's lot. Would you feel comfortable running a business like this? Would you feel like a smart business man?

So what can you do to avoid this unnecessary stress? Again it is just plain simple. Just do the things that you read about in this book. Keep the lines of communication open. Promote teamwork, don't just talk about it. Improve your leadership and show respect to all your employees. And have a passion about what you do, not just for yourself but for everybody. If you do the things that are in this book at an even halfway decent level, you will go a long way to lowering the unnecessary stress in your workplace. And this will cost you will little if any money at all. How much does it cost just to stop and talk to an employee? Pat them on the shoulder, tell them they are doing a nice job, and you are glad to have them working for you. Ask how their family is; ask how they themselves are doing. Shake their hand. Let them know that you actually care about them. That you care about how they feel and how they think. Keep track of their birthdays, anniversaries, and their kids' birthdays. Can you imagine the look on their faces if you brought in a gift for one of their children's birthdays? Can you imagine the look on the child's face when their parent is telling them that the gift is from their boss? All of this only takes a few minutes of your time every day. And will save you so much in the long run that it would be foolish not to do it. And not only that, it will impress your employees to no end, not to mention their families. The six things that it takes to be the best manager on the planet are extremely inexpensive to implement. And they are very costly not to implement.

Let's say that you wish to implement a stop smoking program in your workplace. This is a good idea to implement in any workplace, for it will certainly help you cut down on your health costs. I have worked for several companies that have implemented just such a program. Unfortunately, for those companies the level of stress of their workplaces was way too high. So they ended up with poor results from their programs. They could easily write this off as just poor participation from their employees. There's was nothing more that they could do. They had presented the opportunity for their employees to quit, but they had just not taken advantage of it. What they didn't realize was that the success of the program depended a lot on the stress in the workplace. Every workplace that has a high stress level is going to experience a much lower success rate of its health improvement programs than those that have a lower stress rate. Relieving stress is one reason why people smoke in the first place. So if the companies wanted to be successful with their programs, what they had to do first was to reduce the stress level in the workplace. The lower stress levels that the workplace has, the better results you get from any kind of health program that is implemented in the workplace.

COMFORT LEVEL

When I talk about comfort level, I am talking about how comfortable your employees are with *you*. Understanding comfort level is pretty straightforward. The more comfortable people are with their manager, the better their work tends to be. The more uncomfortable a person is, the more their work suffers. So basically what you are trying to do is to raise the comfort level of your employees. The more comfortable and secure that you can make them feel, the better they are going to produce for you. You can probably think back on your work life and find that you were the most creative and productive when you were comfortable in your work environment and with your manager. That is, you felt secure in your job and you were happy with the people around you. There was better communication and teamwork in that environment. So this is your job as a leader, to put your people in the most comfortable environment that you can. If you and I are happy when we go to work in the morning we usually do a better job at work that day. If you go to work and you know that there's going to be infighting and bickering and a general lack of communication among other things going on in the workplace that day, the less that you will look forward to going to work. And when you do go to work, your productivity and happiness will suffer. And if the employee's happiness and productivity suffer, so does the company's. Is that good business?

Basically you want to make your employees feel as secure and comfortable in their work environment as you possibly can. Since everything in this book ties in with everything else in this book, all you have to do is do all the different things that I talk about in this book. You make sure that communication is top-notch. You make sure that there are no walls dividing groups of people. You make sure that your employees know that if they run into a problem that they can bring it to you and you will either solve that problem or you will find someone that can solve it for them. That goes for personal problems as well. Your employees have to be able to count on you 100 percent. The more you employees can count on you, the more comfortable they are going to be in their job. And like I said before, they will be more productive and more creative. The more productive and creative you employees are, the more you win on all levels of your business. The company wins, the customer wins, the other employees win, and you win. That's four impressive wins in one shot. How many managers have you been around in your work life that have been able to pull that off? Why don't you be the one that can pull that off?

If you think of a person in terms of a cylinder, with the cylinder containing all that is a person. The cylinder contains all the hopes and dreams, creativity, happiness, innovations, teamwork, communication etc. etc. that exist in a person at work. The bottom of the cylinder represents the lowest level of the person's productivity. The top of the cylinder represents all of the person's productivity. The higher you raise the comfort level of the employee, the more you obtain from your employee. It is that straightforward to understand. Unfortunately, most managers have the comfort level so low that they miss out on the best part of their employees. They are usually getting around 30-40% on the average from an employee. They wonder why they are always getting the same complaints from their employees about communication, teamwork, favoritism, and so on and so on. There is something wrong in that managers approach to the comfort level of his employees. The manager almost never stops to see if he is making a mistake in his approach to the job he does. And yet he continues to get the same red flag over and over.

This is a good place for your disinterested third person to show up. Again a simple little polling of your people would go a long way to getting the information that you need. Once you get the information all you need to do is make some positive adjustments. The next time you check in with your employees you should notice the results right away. A little help here would save you an enormous amount of trouble. Why put up with problems that can be solved so easily?

I worked for a company once that would do a survey every year to see how they were doing living up to the basic core values of their business. They would give out surveys to everyone of their employees in the company. On the survey were questions to rate how well they lived up to their core values. There were two parts to every question. The first part of the question was to assign a number from 1 to 5 on how well the company lived up to these values. The second part of the question was for comments on how the company lived up to their values. This was an excellent way for the company to find any problems in the way it was managing its people and its company. A person could write down anything that they wanted to, and it would be okay. Unfortunately, this company would not make use of the information that they received. What they would do is they would take the first portion of the each question and turn it into an average number for that question, such as 4.1 being the average. If the 4.1 was higher than the number that they received the last year, they would be happy as a clam at high tide. And yet they would ignore all the comments that they received from their people about the other problems that would keep them from receiving a five on that question. And every year those comments for each question would be almost identical. The same problems over and over again. These were the problems that were defeating the company and its plants. Yet they would happily go on their way thinking that they did a little bit better than last year. The best manager on the planet would have looked over each and every one of those comments to find the problems that he needed to solve next. He would not have been satisfied until he was able to root out each and every one of those problems, and then find a solution for them. The employees of the company were telling them specifically what problems they were having and going even so far as to name names of people who were causing those problems. And yet the company did nothing about them. That is a recipe for failure. If the company had chosen to go after each and every one of those problems that was written down, they would have increased their respect, their communication, their teamwork and their leadership without a doubt. The problems that needed to be solved were actually written down for them and they did nothing at all about them. That is not being a very good manager. That is just a plain unwise road to travel. If you ask the question, then you had better be prepared for the answer. I have met very few managers in my time who were ready to deal with the answers that they found to their questions. If you can't deal with the answer, then do not ask the question. By the way, guess what happened to the company? They *let* themselves be bought out.

Asking questions of your employees is particularly important when you have what is known as an open door policy. An open door policy is simply saying that a manager is available at just about any time for you to come to them with a problem. And they will be more than happy to sit down and listen to that employee's concerns. I can remember the time when there was no such thing as an open door policy. You either liked it or you didn't and that was that. My way or the highway. If you had something to say or had some input on your job, you just kept it to yourself. So having an open door policy is a very good start. Unfortunately, it is only half of the battle. If you have an open door policy, you must also have an *open mind policy*. You need to be able to listen to employees concerns without any preconceived notions whatsoever. If an employee comes to you in an open door policy, even if that employee's concerns are not doable, you must get back to that employee and give them a reason why. That not only keeps the lines of communication open, but it also tells the employee that they can trust you. If they trust you, they will respect you. If they respect you, they will communicate with you better. If they communicate with you better, you will be able to solve more and more of your problems and make your job and the employee's job's that much simpler. You will be able to make your company that much stronger. In this day and age, you need the strongest company that you can. Nobody ever started your company with the expressed desire to be bought out.

Your job as a leader now is simple. You are to seek out and rid the work environment of all the problems that exist in it. If there is no teamwork, you must make sure that teamwork is fixed. If the communication is part of the problem, then you must find a way to make the communication better. If there is bickering between two groups of people, then you must step in and make sure there is no more bickering between the groups of people. You find a solution that satisfies everyone and you move on. Once you rid your environment of a problem, it is very easy to stay on guard and keep it out of your environment for good. Smart managers are always keeping their problems to a minimum. If you keep your problems to a minimum you are going to have a lot more time and energy to tackle any other problems that come your way. If you are dealing with a lot of problems over and over, and a big problem comes your way, you will take the full force of that problem head on. Keeping problems to a minimum allows the team much more flexibility to deal with new problems. There is no need to be continually repeating the same problems over and over. *A group of people working together put a man on the moon.* Are you willing to make a case that states that your teamwork or communication problems are a bigger problem than putting a man on the moon? Just because most work environments tend to have these problems in them does not mean for a second that they need to exist. *A group of people working together put a man on the moon.* Your group of people working together can solve all the problems that you have. You are a leader. You must lead them to finding those solutions as a team. People are depending on you to help find those solutions. Be smart and stay ahead of the curve as best you can.

Let me tell you a secret about being a leader. You are always "on" no matter what you do. Once you step into a leadership position, you are a leader at all times. You cannot run and hide from your responsibilities. You made the choice to be a leader. No one is holding a gun to your head. You have only three choices now as a leader. You can go backward. You can be stagnant. Or you can move forward. Those are the only three choices that you have. No matter what you do, you will be picking one of those three. There is absolutely no getting around that. Since you are already in a management position and you must make a choice, why would you choose anything but going forward? The other two choices have no payoff. As a leader why would you want to choose them? Besides, going forward is where the fun really is. Can you imagine coming to work on any given day, facing little or none of the problems that you face on a daily basis? Can you imagine what you could accomplish? Can you imagine how much fun you could have? Imagine a day with no communication problems, no teamwork problems, no bickering, no infighting, no power plays, no backstabbing or any of the problems that are in a normal workplace? Do you think it would be impossible to have a workplace like that? *A group of people working together put a man on the moon.* Are the problems that your team faces larger than that?

These are the things you do to raise your employee's comfort level at work. And when you raise your employees comfort level, you raise your own comfort level. And let's not leave out your boss. Everyone has a boss, you know. It is always nice that he or she is in their comfort zone. It just makes life are little easier. Smart management. Besides, they might just learn something from you. Now that is what I call a win-win situation.

PROBLEM SOLVING

Another thing that you need to be able to do it is, to be able to solve problems. To be good at problem solving, first and foremost, you must take out any emotion from the problem itself. As long as there is the emotion in the problem while you are trying to solve it, you will make things very difficult for yourself and the team. You must be able to take a problem and look at it in the cold light of day, with nothing attached to it. Basically you must become a Vulcan, like Mr. Spock, to solve your problems. The more logical and unemotional you are when you look at a problem, the better your chances are that you are going to have to solve any problem. Emotion may also include what you *think* about a problem. You may have a problem with another manager in a different team. If you let your emotions interfere with your judgment, you will hinder yourself from solving the problem. By taking the emotion out of a problem, you save yourself from a lot of unnecessary baggage. The less baggage that you have to deal with, the easier it becomes to solve the problem. Besides, by dealing with the other manager without the emotion, you might just discover some new common ground.

You must acquire as much information as possible about any given problem. The more information that you have, the better your chances of success. Let's say you, for instance, that you run a grocery store and you want to run the best grocery store around. Now you could bring in new products. You could try different ways to attract your customers. But a better way would be to gather as much information from your customers as to what they want. The better you can match up to your customers wants and needs, the more successful you will be. Make a questionnaire available at the entrance for all customers, so that they may be able to write down information that would be beneficial to the both of you. They can even take these questionnaires home. If they knew that you would respond to their input, the better your information will become. Basically, you are setting up a team environment between you, your grocery store and the customers. Let them tell you about any problems that they may have with you. You may be doing things wrong and be totally unaware of it. This is a very good way to double check to see if you are not making mistakes that you're unaware of. Information. Information. Gather as much of it as possible. Check with your people to see if there is information they may give you that might be valuable to the performance of the team. Most managers do not bother to acquire the necessary information to raise the level of their performance. They just merrily go about their way, doing it the way it has been done before. Winners do not hang out in these arenas. They are way too busy gathering information and becoming very successful.

There are going people who say that some problems are just too complex to solve. What they are actually doing is saying they don't know how to solve the problem. No matter how complex a problem may seem, the way to solve it is to break it down to its lowest common denominator. Just like algebra. If you continue to look at a problem as complex, you will never be able to solve that problem. You must go to the core common denominator of a problem to solve it. Every problem has a core common denominator to it. All you have to do is find it. If you perceive complex problems from that point of view, you will be able to deal with complex problems. It is all in how you view a problem. Look at a computer, for instance. A computer looks like a very complex machine on the surface. But when you go to the core level of a computer it is nothing more than ones and zeros. It just manipulates these ones and zeros very quickly. But the core of any computer, even a supercomputer, is simply ones and zeros. Machine language. By manipulating the machine language you can make a computer do whatever you want it to do. By bringing a situation down to its core denominator, it becomes much easier to understand that situation. Then it becomes easier to deal with that situation. Just be able to find a common denominator in a situation and you will be able to solve that situation. Things are not always as complex as they seem on the surface.

It does not matter whether you are running a grocery store or a large corporation. Problem solving is the same everywhere you go. Just gather as much information as you possibly can, surround yourself with the best people, have a backup plan in case plan A doesn't workout, and you will be a very successful manager.

THE SINGLE STEP

The difference between winning and losing usually comes down to a single step. That is, you can have everything except for one little piece of the puzzle. I have been around many managers who had it all but they lacked one simple item. And that item would make the difference between being a top notch manager who could command trust, respect, loyalty and teamwork and one who fell into the ranks of the ordinary. One simple step that they did not do would be their undoing. And this single step could be anything. It could be an attitude, or lack of trust or a communication problem.

Let me tell you of a man that I once worked for. He is just one example. It could have been many of the people that I encountered in my life. I'm sure that you have met many people like this yourself. This man seemed to have everything. He was a respected businessman. He made plenty of money. He had a beautiful wife. He had every toy except a lunar rover. In short, on the surface he looked like a poster child for the American Dream. There was only one problem. He not only thought he was better than other people, but he made the mistake of showing it. That one mistake was his undoing. A single step. It made all the difference in the world. Had he been able to see how fortunate he was to have what he had, to appreciate it for what it was, he would have made that single step to true success. If he had made that single step, he would have had it all. The whole package. The whole enchilada. He would have been nearly invincible in business. His people would have brought out their best for him. Instead, what he got was ordinary. His workplace looked, felt and acted ordinary. The difference between being one of the few and one of the many is but a single step. How many people have you known in your life that fit into this profile? How many managers have you been around that were only one step away from having it all? I'm not talking about the toys; I'm talking about the success. I have been around so many managers that worked in a great business, had good people working for them and still they would not take that single step to become great. Most never even knew that they were that close to greatness. Some knew, but were afraid to take that final step.

That single step is the difference between winning it all, and merely getting by. Most of us know who Tiger Woods is and his pumping of his fist when he sinks that final shot on a hole. How many of you have felt that way when you walked out the door from work at the end of the day? Not many, I'll bet. You can, you know. By making that final step as a manager you can go from an ordinary day at work to the best feeling you can imagine at work.

We sit at home and watch the Super Bowl, NBA finals or the World Series and see the team that wins with all their joy and jubilation. We think it is only for them to enjoy a feeling from their job like that. Well, I'm here to tell you that you can have the feeling as well. I've seen it done. I've done it myself. It is available to anyone who wants it. Do the things that I talk about in this book, add what you want to it, and take that final step and all will be yours. What is your gain is also your peoples' gain, the company's gain and the customers gain. Who said management couldn't be exciting? It is all up to you. It is your choice. The information for your success is all around you. All you have to do now is reach out and grab it. I'll be rooting for you all the way. And I mean all the way!

CHAPTER 2

▼

RESPECT

Respect is the most important part of your foundation of being a leader. You absolutely have to have respect to do your job as a leader. Without respect in your job as a leader you can only *dictate*. That's why they refer to those kinds of people as dictators. They don't lead, they *tell* people what to do. Do you want to go through your working life as a dictator? I certainly hope not.

So, what is respect? Basically are two types of respect. There is the respect that comes *with* your job, and there's the respect that you *earn*. The first respect, the respect that comes with your job, has mainly to do with your being able to hire and fire people or at the very least, get people hired and fired. It also has to do with your influence on people's pay. Or even perhaps what job they may do at work. Most other managers that I have been around lived and died by this type of respect. Mainly they died by it. And the reason that they died by it was, because they thought that was the only respect to that they needed to know about. Unfortunately they did not pay any attention to the respect that you earn. They would usually think that they were due respect mainly because they were in charge. "I am better than you are and therefore you must show me respect". They thought that that alone was supposed to be enough to command respect from their people. I am sure that you have been around plenty of individuals like this. Unfortunately looking at respect from this angle is a very weak and inefficient way of understanding respect. This is the type of respect that is used by dictators. "You had better respect me or else" is what they say. And they usually can back it up. The best manager on the planet has no use for this attitude at all. He knows there is a much better way of accomplishing the task. He knows that true leadership is *always* going to win the day.

The second respect, the earned respect, is the respect of winners not dictators. You earn people's respect by doing all the things I talk about in this book. But basically it can be summed up in a single sentence. *Lead by example.* Most managers fail because they basically tell people by their actions, to do as they say, not do as they do. And that kind of thinking will destroy your ability to manage people almost every single time. From then on, people will only smile and tell you what you want to hear. And if you continue to build on this failure, your whole tenure as a manager will be an illusion of success at best. You will go through life thinking you were successful, when in fact you were a failure as a manager. Does this sound familiar?

It is time to stop here and talk about something very important. Especially to you. Namely, *your* life. If you go through your life living an illusion as to who and what you are, you will end up wasting your life. Is that a choice you wish to make? And I say choice because you do have a choice. You do not have to live your life as an illusion. You do not have to go down the same path in life as others have done. You do not have to do everything the way it's always been done before, just because that's the way it's always been done. You now have a choice, to break out of that and follow a new path. The road less traveled. It is quite possible to go through life and have all the trappings of success. You can have a nice job; you can have a nice house, the great car and the great retirement. And to some people that means that they have been successful. However, that in no way, shape or form implies success. The old way of doing things is quite content to reward people to continually be doing things the old way. You have all heard the stories about not making waves, don't rock the boat and so on and so forth. Well, no one is asking you to make waves. What I am asking you to do is to take a long hard look at the way things have been done. Since this is your one and only life, you need to ask yourself a question. Do I want to spend the rest of my life doing something that may have questionable results in reality? What if the way things are generally done is actually very inefficient? Remember, this is *your* life. You are ultimately responsible for how you live your life, because you see, respect starts with you! If you do not respect yourself, how can anyone else respect you? If you do not treat yourself with respect, how can you treat others with respect?

I once worked with a manager that wanted more than anything else to be liked. He wanted everybody to like him. And everyone did. He was a really nice guy. Unfortunately, little did he know that no one respected him. Or more to the point, no one respected his decision-making. But everyone liked him. And he would come to work every day happy in the fact that everyone liked him. And by doing this he created an Illusion about his abilities. He rarely saw his mistakes. Nor would he understand his mistakes if he saw them. His main concern was that he was liked. And because of that, he was blind to everything else. I have no doubts that this man will go to his grave happy in the fact that everyone liked him. He has all the trappings of success. He has the car, the house, etc. etc. But, he will never be a successful manager. At the real job of managing his plants and his people, he did a very poor job. Because he never stopped to take a look around himself and do a reality check. And whenever there was a real problem to deal with, he didn't even know what was going on. Too bad he didn't have a person that he could have checked in with. If he had stopped to do a reality check, he would have saved himself a whole lot of trouble. I guarantee you, you do not want to get to the end of your life and find out you wasted it. Before you say that this life is yours to waste, remember that you are part of a team. People depend on you and you depend on them. You only get to waste your life on your own time.

Let me give you an example about missing out on a chance to earn some respect. The company that this man works for decided to implement some new software that would more efficiently do the business of the company. Now this new software was really pretty good.

Unfortunately, it was a very complicated program and as such had a steep learning curve. Now some of his people who would be using that program made some calls to some other plants that had already implemented that program, to find out what may becoming their way. Sort of checking ahead of time to see what problems they might be facing. Smart thinking. Everyone told them that they would be looking at a 6 to 9 mos. learning curve. So when the software came to their plants, instead of getting all of the training that was necessary to input the information into the software, what they got was 90 minutes of training on a Friday afternoon. The new software was to go live Sunday morning. As you can see, a major problem was coming. Not only were the people unprepared to implement the new software, the company was not going to run the old software in parallel just in case there was a problem. You can guess what happened. The plant came to a standstill. This plant that the manager was in charge of went from being the best in the company to the worst in one weekend. Customers who had come to depend on this plant without question were now calling in in anger as to where their shipments were. It was one of the largest management mistakes that I had ever seen. And guess where that manager was at? On vacation. Sound like anybody you ever worked for? Not only did he not pay any attention to his employees concerns, but he never bothered to check to see what kind of problems this new software would pose for him and his plants. He just was not on top of the situation. You do not earn your employees respect by not hearing their concerns. There's a difference between listening and hearing. Hearing means to understand what a person is saying. Even if no one had voiced any concerns, he should have been prepared for what was coming. If his people saw it, why didn't he? Don't walk out in front of a truck, just because you are not paying attention.

So what should this manager have done? Simple. He should have *heard* his employees concerns. He should have checked out the problem that was headed his way. There was more than enough information available to him to be to get a handle on the situation. Even if he could not have solved the problem totally, and effort on his part would have been greatly appreciated. He would have earned respect for that alone. Always remember this: Your employees will not respect you in the morning after you have screwed them. Always stay on top of your problems. Gather as much information as you possibly can, and then do your absolute best to solve the problems. Then you can go on vacation.

This is a good place to stop and talk about something very important. To find out how good a manager is, you find out how they do in a very difficult situation. The measure of a good manager is their ability to handle tough situations. Any manager can look sharp when the going is good. However, when the going gets rough, that's when you find out just how good a manager really is. In the preceding story, the managers had all the information about a problem that was headed their way. They had good people around them, they had the ability to gather the necessary information to deal with a problem and yet they totally dropped the ball on it. This will not impress your employees. This will not impress your boss. How you perform when the stuff hits the fan, is the real measure of your ability to manage people. You cannot drop the ball or blame your employees. Nobody is asking you to be perfect.

However, you are expected to deal with the situation. This is where you bring to bear all the information that you learn from this book or anywhere else you have picked up any information. If you apply what is in this book to your situation, you will be able to take the majority of the wind out of the problem. Then, what was a very big problem will become a much smaller problem and one that is so much easier to manage. By doing it this way you will impress the hell out of your employees. This is one of the very best ways to earn respect from your employees. Learn how to prepare for and handle tough situations. Gather as much information as you can. Get your employees involved as soon as you can. Make sure all lines of communication are open. Get as much feedback from your employees as you can. Make sure that any other groups that are to be involved are also on line and are on the same page as everyone else. Prepare. Prepare. Solve as many of the logistic problems as you can foresee. But most of all get a winners' mindset going in every single person involved. Success or failure is in the *preparation*. If you wait for the problem to arrive, you will fail almost every single time.

Respect is absolutely paramount in your job. Without respect you can only dictate, never lead. The manager I just mentioned earlier wanted mainly to be liked. If he had done his job properly, he would have been respected *and* liked. He would have had the best of both worlds. But he ended up with much less. Do you wish to settle for less? Is your life so unimportant that you would settle for less when you do not have to?

And here is something else about respect. If your people respect you for the job that you do as a manager, they would gladly follow you into the gates of hell itself. But they will not be following you so much, but for that which you stand for. What do you stand for as a manager? I mean in reality, not what you *think* you stand for. Remember, you can think anything; it's what you can back up that ultimately counts. So be very careful in your assessment of yourself. A mistake here can go on and on. A mistake that goes on and on breeds more mistakes. Mistakes that breed will do nothing to raise your level of respect or happiness.

I knew a manager once that whenever it his employees would come to him with a problem that he felt was too small for him to deal with, he would say to them "tomorrow is another day". Now by doing this, this manager was destroying any respect his employees might have had for him. That is not something you wish to say your employ-ees. You never brush anything off as trivial. And not only did that manager make that mistake, but he made another one also. Tomorrow was not going to be another day. All the people that were in today and had screwed it up were going to be in tomorrow. Tomorrow was not going to be a different day. Tomorrow was going to be just like today. And his employees knew that. Groundhog Day over and over. Unfortunately, this manager made two big mistakes and didn't even notice it. Guess what happened to him? He was promoted.

It is so much easier to stay on top of things that it is to let them slide. If you do all the little things on a daily basis, keeping the lines of communication open, listening to your employees needs and keeping an eye on the big picture, you are going to be so much better off. Most of the man-agers and I have been around in 35 years of working have spent very little if any time at all earning people's respect. What a huge opportunity these people missed out on.

Once you start trying some of this, you are going to notice the difference almost immediately. It will take a while for your people to adjust to you. But don't give up.

Do you know that most of your employees expect you to *fail?* That's right, as a manager your employees expect you to be a failure. Just about every manager they have seen has done a poor job. And I mean a poor job compared to the job they could have been doing. There is a world of difference between the two. It is a very sad state of affairs when your employees expect you to fail or at the very least expect you to do a mediocre job. If you are coming to work and start doing all of things that are talked about in this book, you would absolutely amaze your employees. If I knew when I went to work that I was expected to fail or to do a mediocre job, I would be one pissed off person. I guarantee you that would be the very last thing that I would do. Failure would not be an option. I would gather as much information on doing the job of management as I could possibly beg, borrow or steal. Nothing but nothing would stop me from being the best. And that is the way it should be with you. Do you want to be looked at as a failure, a mediocre manager or just a general pain in the butt for all your working life? Most employees think of a new manager as simply "what do I have to put up with now to do my job". They are not expecting a top-notch manager to show up for work on any given day. Or for that matter, at any time during their working lives. They are usually not even expecting a good manager to show up. While unfortunately that is a sad commentary on the state of affairs of management today, the flip side is, it opens up a huge opportunity for you. Why don't you step up and be a top-notch manager? Why don't you go to work tomorrow and start knocking people's socks off? Get up in the morning and shake your fist of the sky and say "I'll be damned if I'll be a failure or be mediocre today". Let the sky know that you are coming to work and you will not fail! Like I said at the beginning, I am going to be brutally honest with you. That is the only way that we are going to get where we want to go. I do not want you to be mediocre during your working life. I probably will never meet you in this life, but that does not mean for a second that I do not care about you. You have a great opportunity to change your little corner of the world. That is not only important to me, but to everybody on this planet. Can you imagine what the world would be like if everyone took care of their own little corner of the world? Do not ever underestimate your importance at any time during your life. Just don't let it go to your head.

CHAPTER 3

▼

COMMUNICATION

Communication is another building block in your foundation as the best manager on the planet. At almost every job that I have worked at in my life, communication has been a problem. I'll bet that you are experiencing it right now. Like I said the previous chapter, people listen but they do not hear. Quality communication is much more than just hearing. It can be body language or something as simple as a smile or a pat on the back.

Here is your chance to really have some fun. Improving communication is one of the easiest ways for you and your employees to have fun. This is where you go out and mingle with your employees. You can go out and pat them on the back and tell them what a great job they are doing. You can tell them that you are proud to working with them. This is the place you can go and make the biggest changes so easily. When was the last time you went to a really fun meeting? Most meetings and I have been to have been boring and repetitious to say the least. Here is a good chance for you to change course. When you have your team meetings, decide to have fun. Bring in a cake, or ice cream or a pie and just relax. Start off by telling some jokes. Put your people in a relaxed frame of mind. Try letting one of your employees lead the meeting. Sit back and let your employees run the whole show for once. You just might be pleasantly surprised. There are just all kinds of things that you can do to spice up a meeting to make it more fun and enjoyable for everyone. Meetings do not have to be dull. It is not cast in stone that meetings have to be dull. Look around. There is all kinds of information about the way the other people do to break the mold. Be innovative. Do some research. A little nosing around on your part can reap great rewards in dealing with meetings.

Everyone has horror stories about meetings that they have attended. Let me tell you about one that I went to. The meeting was with two different groups of people and was presided over by the plant manager. The meetings started off with the manager's of the two groups arguing with each other. Standing up and waving their fingers at each other, no less. While this was happening, the plant manager did nothing at all. Not only were the two managers looking less than competent as managers, but they were communicating something else to the groups. By arguing, the two managers were telling everyone else that it was ok to argue with each other. After all, their leaders were leading them into the direction of arguing with each other. Then, to top it off, the two managers would wonder why their two teams never got along. Teamwork and communication were negatively impacted. Not only did they look foolish, but they sent a message to the teams that was detrimental not only to the workings of the teams but as to the plant as a whole. And to top it off again the plant manager, by doing nothing, merely reinforced that communication. A simple little meeting on the surface, turned out to be much, much more than that. Like I said before, you are always on. Be very careful of what you are communicating. Do not repeat the mistakes of these managers.

Communication is an ongoing and daily task. It is something that you are doing all of the time. If I spent all of my time in the office and do very little mingling with my employees, I could easily be communicating a number of different things. Almost all of them negative. Remember, you are always "on" no matter what you think. People are social beings. And as such, they need contact with other human beings most of the time. If you are sitting your office, you could very well be saying to your people that you do not care about them, or what you care about what they do at their job. If you are overwhelmed with paperwork at your job, and you must spend almost all of your time in your office, then you had better find a way to communicate with your employees off the job. Remember, you are out to be the best. So you must find ways to solve problems if the standard ways are not available to you. Winners always have a plan B. And they usually have a plan C and D. So if anything ever goes wrong with plan A, they are ready to implement plan B. Never miss a beat.

You must always be looking for ways to improve the lines of communication within your group. Try to mingle with your employees on a daily basis. Just walk around. Pat them on the shoulder. Tell them a funny joke that you have heard. Ask them how things are going. If you are truly doing your job as a manager and looking to improve the lines of communication, teamwork and respect in your team, then all kinds of useful information about the team will becoming to you. All it takes is a little bit of work. Always strive to keep your communication "bone honest". The information you get from your employees has to be totally honest. You have got to be able to let your people tell you absolutely anything about the working environment. And when they can tell you anything about the work environment, they will tell you about any personal problems that they might have and feel comfortable doing so. Off the job problems can negatively impact the employee and the work environment. A little bit of work that will bring you huge rewards. Good investors in the stock market are happy if they receive 20 percent a year on their investments. A good manager can get returns far higher than that just by doing a few simple things on a daily basis at his or her job. And there is no risk whatsoever. Now that is smart thinking. No risk, high returns. What investor in the stock market would not want to have that deal? It is all up to you. All you have to do is make the conscious choice to go out and make the communication in your team better. Not only will your communication improve, but you will be solving problems for the team, the company and the customers. Problems that other managers will choose to ignore and therefore help to defeat themselves, their employees and their company.

Like I said earlier in the book, you need to have an open door policy coupled with an open mind policy. You must make your employees comfortable in the fact that they can come into your office at any time and discuss anything at all with you, and feel safe in doing so. Only then will you truly make progress. This is part of being the best manager on the planet. This is part of being a smart manager. If you do not do these kinds of things, you are just asking for trouble. Would you consciously want to ask for trouble? Is that something that you would find appealing?

Let's say that one of your employees has a serious personal problem off the job. A problem like that can be trouble to an individual and also bring trouble into your workplace. If you have excellent lines of communication, you will be able to sit down with an employee and figure out a solution for them. If you cannot find a solution for them, you must be able to find someone else that can help them. You must not write off people's problems as something you do not wish to deal with. If it is something that affects your workplace, then it is something that you must deal with, whether you like it or not. If you are on top of your lines of communication, you will be able to deal with this problem as easily as possible. If you had been moving throughout your group on a daily basis, you would find out about these kinds of problems long before they became problems for you and your team. That is smart management. Having great communication in your team rewards you and your employees on many levels at the same time. Being a great manager is so much easier than not being one. And, it is a lot more fun. Why do things the hard way, when you do not have to do them that way? Playing to win is much easier than playing to lose. Don't play to lose.

Here is something else that you can do to make communication easier for you and your employees. Find out what each of your employees likes to do as a hobby. If one of your employees likes to fish, then go fishing with them sometime. When was the last time to that your boss did something like that with you? It not only opens up the lines of communication, but it also wins on other levels as well. You build respect with that individual as well as opening up your lines of communication better. If an employee likes to do something that you have very little knowledge of, then you also get to learn something new at the same time. Now you are really starting to win. Do not write these seeming little ideas off until you try them. Even though I do not know you, I have a vested interest in seeing you succeed. Everything that makes you better makes us all better. Think like a winner, and you will become a winner. Couple that with a never say die attitude, and life will reward you. Life loves winners.

Communication is the arena where you solve your problems. Problems are like bills. If for some reason you cannot pay your bills from month to month the quality of your life and your family's life will be impacted negatively. If you pay your bills on a regular basis each month, and have money left over for other things in your life, your life is a whole lot different than those who are always dealing with a mountain of bills. If you have too many bills to deal with each month you put an enormous amount to pressure on yourself and your family. The life that you live is a lot different from the one that you have when you pay all your bills on time and have money left over. If you do not solve your problems on a timely basis, you'll soon be dealing with so many problems that you will be overwhelmed most of the time. Your ability to do your job, to think properly and to feel good, will be impacted negatively. I am sure that you have noticed by this stage in your life, that if you do not solve problems, they soon pile up and become a larger burden for you. Every day it seems that a new problem arises in our life. So if you do not learn to solve problems you can see mathematically that they are just going to pile up on you and overwhelm you. The solution is obvious. You must be able to stay on top of your problems in order for everyone to do their job properly on a day-to-day basis. This is where communication comes in.

Let me give you an example with a place that a friend of mine at. When he went to work for this company, is seem like a pretty nice company on the surface. After being there for a while it became evident to him they had the standard problems that most companies seem to have. Poor communication, no teamwork between departments, in fighting, back biting, and the assorted other problems that go along with the company that has disarray amongst its people. You have probably worked at a place just like this in your past or may be doing so right now. A place that is basically a pain in the ass to go to work.

What the company wanted to do was to grow and become a bigger company. Unfortunately, they had so many internal problems that they were making it unduly harsh on themselves to do just that. So here's what he did. Even though he initiated it, it was the team that provided the solutions. First of all, he went to each group and asked them a simple question, "Do you like doing things the hard way every day at your job"? That sentence was going to be the one that was the center of how they solved their problems. Hopefully nobody wants to come to work every day and do things the hardest way possible. So if they understand up front that what they're doing to solve problems is going to make their job easier and better, your work is going to get much better results. Then he had each department list each problem that it had to deal with on a daily basis. Actually, any problem that they had to confront continually while trying to do their job. This is important because it gets the problems out in the open now. Problems that are written down and can be viewed over and over are problems that they can begin to deal with. It makes the problem solid. It is no longer something that is whispered or said as a phrase or a sentence that disappears after it is said. By writing a problem down they could keep it in the open and have a much better chance of solving that problem.

The next step is to organize the problems on a board. I am talking about a single place for all your problems to be written down, so that everybody may view them at any time. Now the problems have become visible. And by being visible, they were going to be so much easier to deal with and gotten rid of. When he asked everybody what problems they had to deal with, he also asked them to put down some solutions they thought would solve the problems. Communicating problems is not just a bitch session. It is about finding out the problem *and* the solution, and then removing the problem from your work life. As a manager you cannot be expected to solve all the problems yourself. That is just not fair. It has to be a team effort. However, as a manager you must lead people to a situation that allows them all to start solving their problems.

Now that they had their problems written down, they could start wiping them out to one by one. They took the problems that caused them the most problems by itself and dealt with those first. You want to get as many of the big problems out of the way as soon as you can. This accomplished two different things. First, they got some major problems out of the way right away. Secondly, it shows the teams that they could trust and respect him. Once they could see that he was making things happen, and then the situation of solving the problems really began to take off. Basically what he was was a choreographer. He was the one who was going to be going around and making sure that the solutions that have been implemented were working and continued to work. He was like a large umbrella. He covered all the teams to make sure that the solutions were being implemented properly. A lot of managers drop the ball right here. They may come up with a solution, but they fail to follow it through. It is good that they started a solution to a problem; however, they still will be failing because they do not make sure that the solution not only is working but continues to work. This is where one-on-one communication really comes into play. You have got to be walking around and talking to people to find out how everything is really going. Do not rely on the numbers in your computer. They are only half of it. The other half is communication. One-on-one communication is really a whole lot of fun. Make solving the problems fun. Walk around; put your hand on people shoulders. Ask them how is it *really* going? Once people start opening up to you, you'll have all the information that you need. And you are having fun at the same time. A win-win situation.

Once we got some of our major problems out of the way, not only did our jobs become more enjoyable, but we could now turn our attention to the smaller problems. Our customers, our vendors and anybody that dealt with us noticed the change for the better. We were on the road to having a winning environment. Sales went up. Margins got better. Work became more fun to do than it had before. Teamwork between groups got better. Everything got better across the board. And it all started with communication. Now it is your turn. Make it happen in your workplace. Get out there and start having some fun.

CHAPTER 4

▼

LEADERSHIP

When I was in the service, I went to school at Fort Benning, Georgia. At Fort Benning there is a school for officers called Officers Candidate School. This is where they trained their officers to send off to war. The patch that these officers wore on their jackets had two words on it. Follow me! Those two words summed up what it was to be a leader. Follow me! That is leadership in a nutshell.

I am going to repeat some things I talked about earlier in the book. It is simply because they bear repeating. You can not talk about leadership without talking about communication. You can not talk about communication without talking about respect. If you want to your people to communicate better, then you must lead them to better communication. If you want better teamwork in your people, then you have to lead them to teamwork. If you want higher morale in your people, then you must lead them to higher morale. Now you may say that you do not really want to do that. Unfortunately you have no choice. You are always "on" as a leader no matter what. If you have a leadership position you cannot hide from leading. You have chosen to take the job on your own accord. Nobody held a gun to your head. Now maybe you would rather do it like it's always been done before because it seems easier that way. Let me give you an example of what happens when you just blindly follow the old ways. I once worked for a company that had a "hands off" management policy. On the surface this sounded pretty good. They would *empower* their people to make their own decisions. Sounded really good. Empower their people. Unfortunately, the reality was quite different. What it turned into was a situation where no manager took responsibility for anything. They wanted to have all the glory of being a manager without doing any of the work. They became the laughing stock of the company. Their people would always smile and tell them what they wanted to hear. But when they turned their backs and walked away, the people laughed at who the managers really were. The managers sold themselves out. By not being leaders, they made a mockery of their own lives. There is no such thing as "hands off" management. You are either a manager or you are not. The sooner you come to grips with this reality, the better off you and your people and your company are going to be. This is your one and only life! You do not want to waste it. People are counting on you to step up and do your job. But like I have said before, it is easier and better to do it this way than it is to do it "the way it's always been done". Especially when "the way it's always been done" yields such poor results. We are talking about being the best manager on the planet. Play to win!

A leader is someone who is active in their approach to the job at hand. A leader is someone was is moving their group, no matter how large or small, in a positive direction. They are people who do not come to their office and sit back and look through the window of their office at their employees. They are people who are out on the floor actively engaging their employees at every chance they get. You did you won't find leader's "sucking up" in the bosses office. They do not have time for that nonsense. They know that their job is to raise the comfort level of employees every chance they get. They know that being actively engaged with their employees in a positive manner; they will be accomplishing their mission statement and making their company a stronger and more viable competitor in this highly competitive business world.

So many managers make the mistake of thinking that their employees should be the source of all their solutions. That is simply not true. You as a leader must lead them to the source. It must come from you, because it will not come from anywhere else. It may come from your employees, but it will be because you gave them the opportunity with your leadership to do so. If you want your employees to have better teamwork, you must display teamwork yourself. If you want better communication in your workplace, then you must be a better communicator yourself. What ever you'll want from your employees you must be willing to get from yourself. You must lead by example! Do not ever try to lead by talking, that will lead you nowhere. How many managers can you find in your past that actually lead by example? How many of them were great communicator's? How many of them were really good team players? How many of them showed an outstanding respect for you? And so on and so on. The answer is that very few do. It is really simple to be a good manager. Just bring it out in yourself and everything else will fall into place. All the information you need is all around you. All you have to do is go get it. It has all been solved before.

A friend of mine had a son that was diagnosed in the second grade as having a learning disorder. Now my friend, who had attended very good schools when he was growing up, believed that the school was telling him the right thing with their diagnosis. What the school proposed was that his son be put in a special education class. By putting his son in a special education class, his son could receive the extra education that he needed to bring him up to speed with his peer group. So, my friend agreed to allow the school to put his son in a special education class. Everything seemed fine on the surface. Unfortunately, the reality of the situation was going to be very different. You would think that if a child was behind in school, that by giving him special education you would be able to bring that child up to the speed of his peers. Unfortunately, for the father and son, this "special education" would result in the son falling farther and farther behind each year he went to school. Instead of speeding the child up and bringing him up to speed with his peer group, he was actually falling farther and farther behind. When the father went to the school to see why his son was falling farther behind each year, what he saw was they were actually making no effort to help his son at all. For example, when he went to his son's math class at school, the multiplication tables were posted on the wall. The school was not even getting the children in the class to memorize the multiplication tables. In fact, they were doing none of the work that you would think that would needed to be done to bring a child up to speed. When was the last time you went into a store and they have the multiplication tables posted on the wall so that you could figure out your purchases? What the school was actually doing was increasing the problem that the child had. There was leadership going on here, but it was not the kind of leadership that was having a positive effect.

This is just another case of poor lines of thinking that when used without any kind of double check would cause not only poor leadership on the part of the school, but would have devastating consequences for the children. All because nobody bothered to check to see if all was working like it was supposed to be. Now my friend and his son will have to deal with the consequences for most, if not all their lives. A very sad epitaph for leadership going in the wrong direction. However, my friend happened to be a manager, and a good one at that, so he was able to take this situation and turn it into a positive one for him and his son in the end. That's what good managers can do.

I could go on and on and on with different stories about poor leadership. I am sure that you have plenty of your own. The bottom line is simple. You absolutely have to check out your lines of thinking to make sure that they are actually working. You cannot do your work based on opinions or half-truths. You can see that by not checking out your line of thinking that the consequences can be poor if not downright devastating, if you fail to make sure that what you are using is actually working the way you wanted to. In the last example with the school, if they had polled their teachers and the parents with a simple questionnaire and then poured over all the results that they had gotten, they would have had plenty of information to point them in the right direction. But they made the same mistake that so many managers do. They *assumed* they knew what they were doing. However, the results did not back them up at all. They refused to believe that what they were doing was not working the way that it was supposed to. Do not *assume* anything. Check it out. If you check out what you are doing, just by doing that alone, you will be far ahead of any other manager around you. It is something that is very simple and easy to do. And by not doing it, you open yourself up and the people that depend on you, to enormous problems. Do not do that. A little bit of checking on your part will pay huge dividends to you and all those that depend on you.

ONE DIMENSIONAL MANAGERS

To end this chapter on leadership, I wish to tell you of about a big problem that you're going to have dealing with other managers. This person is what I call a one-dimensional manager. You have probably already run into managers just like this in your work. A one-dimensional manager is basically a manager who only has one side to them. These managers may do things completely different from each other, but they have an awful lot of things in common. They may be dictatorial managers, they may be hands-off managers, they may be self-centered managers or they could be managers that don't seem to have a clue what they're doing. The first thing that these managers have in common is they are just a one trick pony. That is, they only have one way of dealing with a situation. Having only one way of dealing with a situation will put you in a very precarious situation. Life and work are much more complex than that. To have only one way of dealing with situations does not give you the flexibility that you need to be to be a top-notch manager. So many managers will go through their working lives with basically only one way of dealing with situations. These managers generally are not too much fun to work with because they are not able to provide the leadership that it takes to deal with the many different situations that evolve in the workplace. To be a top-notch manager you must be able to vary your style to fit any given situation that arises in your workplace. The more flexibility that you have and the more ability to deal with so many different kinds of situations that you encounter in the workplace, will put to any much better position to be a manager that can handle the job at a first-class level. Let's take a hyper-control manager for instance. This manager wishes to control of everything that is going on in the workplace. They are constantly meddling in other people's jobs. They believe that they are the only ones that have all the knowledge to solve all problems. Unfortunately, the problem with the micromanagement manager is that they are insecure in their abilities. They are bringing their insecurities as a person or a manager to their job. If they trusted other people to do their job, they would not be micromanaging those people. A microman-ager is merely a person who needs to deal with their inse-curities off the job. Then and only then, can they begin to do their job as a real manager. On the other end of the spectrum, the hands-off manager wishes to push the responsibility off onto his or her employees. They basically want to be out of the loop as much as possible. However, when pats on the back are handed out, you can bet they will be first in line. This manager brings absolutely minimal leadership to the table. He will not be able to rise to the occasion when the going gets tough.

Another problem with these types of managers is they tend to get mad or flustered way too often. Anything that does not fit into their one-dimensional way of doing things causes them problems. And anything that causes these managers problems makes them mad or frustrated. There is an old saying that goes "You never get mad at anyone else. You get mad at yourself, but you take it out on others". These managers, unfortunately, live up to that saying. If you are a first-class manager, getting mad at a situation or an employee should be well down on your list. You should have so many different ways of dealing with situations (plan A, plan B, plan C and so on) that you should be able to buffer just about any situation that comes your way. A multidimensional manager is what you wish to become. This manager is not a one trick pony. Nobody is expecting you to be Superman. But by being a multidimensional manager, you will be able to handle so much more than a one-dimensional manager could ever dream of. The trick is to put all the one-dimensional management styles together into a single package. There is a time to be a micromanager. There is a time to be a hands-off manager. By being as multidimensional as possible, you are able to adapt to any given situation that comes your way. Your job will become so much easier and fun than you ever thought possible. It may seem like a lot more work, but that is only on the surface. The more dimensions that you add to your repertoire, the smoother a manager you will become. A multidimensional manager has characteristics like calmness, funny, at ease with them self, confident, pleasant to be around and so on and so forth. But the main characteristic above all else, is when the stuff hits the fan, you can count on this manager 100 percent. You know that he will be there to back you up, not only to the company but to everyone that depends on them. When was the last time that you had a manager that you could count on all of the time? My guess is that is was probably never.

It is absolutely imperative that you become as multidimensional as possible. The more dimensions that you have as a manager gives you more ways of dealing with different situations. If you want to be the best manager on the planet or even just a good manager, you need to have as many dimensions as you possibly can. The information is available to you to improve your ability to handle all different kinds of situations. To not gather that information is a foolish way to do the job. That is inviting defeat into your workplace. There are enough problems in life and the workplace that to openly invite more is just plain foolishness. By being one-dimensional you make your job 100 times harder than it has to be. You would never drive your car with the brakes on. But that is exactly what you do if you come to work with only a one-dimensional attitude.

There are people who say that to be a successful employee you must be able to adapt too many different managers. There is certainly an element of truth to that. That is how most workplaces really are. Later on in this book there is a chapter on critical thinking. I am going to jump ahead here and apply some critical thinking to this situation. The question is, "Is it best to always have your employees adapting to new management styles"? Is that the way that brings out the best in the people and the company? What if we look at this from a different angle? What if *managers* adapted their styles to a single style that worked better? If you are a manager of a group of 20 people, let's say, is it better that 20 employees should adapt to your style or would it be much better for you to adapt a singular style that encompassed everything that a manager should be? Wouldn't it be easier to change your style and bring much more to the table, than to manage a group of people with a style that had so many problems working against it? If a manager adapted a style of management that had all the basics of being a good manager, it would be much more efficient for the manager and the team and the company, than to do it any other way. It is much easier for a manager to adapt a better style of management that it is to ask all the employees to adapt to the managers' style. It not only solves the problem of getting the best out of the team but it also does away with that problem of inefficient management *permanently*. Two birds with one stone. To very large birds, I might add. Like I said at the beginning of the book, this is about winning. This is the way that you play to win. Put your ego aside. Put your inefficient style aside. Adapt a more efficient and multidimensional way of managing people and you will win across the board. This is what being a leader is all about. Being a leader means doing the things that it takes to bring out the best in your self, your employees and your company. Do not waste your time doing anything else. Be a leader. Play to win.

CHAPTER 5

▼

TEAMWORK

Your job as a leader is to lead your people into the best team environment possible. Yet it all of my years in business, I have seen very little real teamwork. What passes for teamwork are usually employees who take it upon themselves to communicate with each other and work together to increase the teamwork between their own jobs. Those employees know that by working together that they can make their jobs a whole lot simpler and easier if they coordinate their work. Managers usually have very little effect on the teamwork that does exist. Usually it is just the opposite. I have only run across a couple of managers who really knew how to make their team work effectively together. Most managers were a hindrance to good teamwork, simply because they failed to understand their jobs properly. To really make teamwork effective is to be able to do all the other things that a leader must do. You must have good lines of communication, you must have earned the respect of your people and you must have shown a certain amount of leadership to begin with. You have to be able to do those things first before you can start attaining real teamwork. Most places have lots of posters on the wall that say great things about teamwork and management does a lot of talking about teamwork. But what ends up really happening is they make a mockery of teamwork by not following through and doing it themselves. Posters and talk are not enough to get it done. That doesn't really add up to anything more than a very ineffective start. If you have the posters and you talk the talk but do not carry through then what happens is you send a message to your employees that they must not "do as you do, but do as you say". That is the basic recipe for failure. You must lead by example. There is no other way. I repeat, there is no other way. You absolutely have to know more about teamwork than anybody else in the group. And if you don't, you had better be learning. You must know what the ebb and flow of the workload is for your group, so that you can continually position your people in the proper places for them to get the job done the most effectively. Lead by example. I cannot say that enough.

There is a law in this universe that you should understand. It is a law that is so simple that very few people actually understand it. And like all laws in this universe you can either go with it or you can go against it. If you should choose to go against it, which an awful lot of people do, then be prepared to pay the price. Nature does not like its laws to be broken. But remember, that as a leader other people will also be paying the price for your mistakes. So be very careful in your choices.

Let's look at gravity first. Gravity keeps us attached to this planet so that we do not go flying off into space. It also keeps the atmosphere intact so that we can breathe. But if you were to jump off a 12 story building gravity would punish you for breaking its rules. Chances are you would not survive your fall. This is just natures' way of telling us not to break her rules. But the law that I really want to talk about is so eloquently shown by the simple hydrogen atom. I picked the hydrogen atom because it is the simplest of all atoms. All other atoms are merely more complicated forms of the simple hydrogen atom. If you understand the simplicity of the hydrogen atom you will understand more than most Heads of State. And that is quite a feat unto itself.

The atom is the basic building block of the universe. Everything that we can see, touch, or taste is made up of atoms. In the center of the hydrogen atom is a proton. It is a positively charged particle. Circling on the outside of the proton is an electron. It is a negatively charged particle. I am sure that most people would agree that the universe that is around us is a pretty fantastic place. And it is all built out of those simple little atoms. Now comes the fun part. The proton is a positive charged particle and the electron is a negative charged particle. *Two opposites working together built this entire universe.* That is what the simple little hydrogen atom is saying to us all. And the existence of the universe screams it at us all. If all the leaders on this planet understood that single sentence, there would be no more war. That's right, no more war. If opposites are working together, there is no reason at all for fighting. This is where your job comes in. You certainly don't control the whole planet, but you do have a certain amount of control over your little piece of the planet. So if you hold up your end of the bargain, and manage your little piece of the planet properly, you are doing your part to make the world a better place to live for all of us. How many people get to say that when they go to work each day? Isn't that something that is worth getting up and going to work for each day? Changing things for the better isn't really that hard. It's doing things that don't work well that are hard.

Teamwork is something that once you get it going, it is easy to keep it going. All you have to do is to get started and the hardest part is over with. This is summed up with Newton's first law of motion, "a body at rest tends to stay at rest, a body in motion tends to stay in motion". Once it is started it takes very little work to keep it going. Unfortunately, a lot of managers do not know much about real teamwork. This country was founded on the premise of the rugged individual. Mainly it was about individuals going out and making it on their own. That was great in the beginning. However, now that our country has been founded, we must switch away from the rugged individualistic thinking to a more teamwork oriented attitude. My father's generation and the generation before him lived through the Great Depression. And as I said earlier in the book about people bringing personal viewpoints into the work environment, this happens to be one of them. Part of what came from this era was that old line of thinking that said "I had to walk to school in the snow, uphill, both ways, 10 miles, with barbed wire wrapped around my bare feet for traction". The people who grew up with this parent would usually find that nothing they did was good enough. It really wasn't the fault of the parents for going through this era; it was just the way things worked out for them. The Great Depression was a very brutal time for a lot of people. I have been around so many managers in my life who thought that other people could never measure up to themselves. That was an offshoot of this line of thinking. Since what they did was never good enough for their father, nobody else was good enough for them. I do not want to single out the fathers, because this line of thinking could be picked up in lots of other places as well. And every parent that lived through this era was not necessarily marked by it. I do not wish to imply that at all. But, by coming to work with this attitude you are in no position whatsoever to accomplish any kind of teamwork. Where did you learn teamwork? Rugged individualism does not teach teamwork very well. This is what I mean by constantly checking out you ways of doing things. It is so much easier to check your lines of thinking out, than it is to just run with them. Think smart. Live and work smart.

What most of these people were really looking for was respect. Respect for who they were and what they could accomplish. Treating others as somehow inferior to themselves is again a recipe for disaster. It appears the easiest way, but in reality it is not. If you truly do want respect, then you must not repeat the mistakes of the past. Stop doing things that do not work. Get them out of your life for good. Once they are gone, you do not have to deal with them anymore. Doing that will really increase your efficiency. Winners are always trying to increase their efficiency.

Here is something else that you can do that will also help your teamwork and efficiency. Get your team involved in the community. Find some projects in the community that you can bring your team into and help to make a difference. It not only helps with your teamwork but also adds a new dimension to your work. Now your team is more than itself. It is part of the larger community that is around it. There is a great payoff to actually working within your community and feeling like you are a part of it, rather than just going to work each day. It does not have to be much at all. Maybe everyone can go down to the park and help clean it up. Maybe there's a soup kitchen that could use a little help. It does not have to be something that is very large at all. It is not the size of the project; it is merely the fact that your people are involved in something other than their job, while at the same time they're working with their own team. It is simple, but will provide you and the team with a very good payoff. It is one thing to find acceptance in a team. It is something else altogether to find acceptance in the team and the community at the same time. This is another place where winners like to hang out. Why don't you?

In the last chapter we talked about leadership. Like I said in the beginning of the book, everything that we are dealing with is interconnected. You can't have one without the other. You lead your people into teamwork. You are beginning to understand that two opposites working together created this entire universe. This can also be summed up by the Chinese picture of the yin and yang. Two opposites in harmony are really what make the world go around. This is such as simple statement. And yet by not understanding that simple statement, we bring upon ourselves so many problems. And all these problems could be avoided. All of them. The hydrogen atom, the yin and the yang, they are the core rule in teamwork.

There are a lot of problems in this country of ours. And behind all of our problems is a lack of teamwork. This country has too much "me me" thinking in it. The lobbyists' line up in the halls of Congress to get what is only beneficial to the companies that they represent. The drug companies only do what is best for them and not what is best for us all. I am not saying that companies should not be able to make their profits, far from it. But if we all worked together first as a team rather than individuals or groups, we could have the best of both worlds. This is not naive thinking. This is the reality of the universe that we all live in. People and groups working together can have it as best as it possibly can be. And to get there we need leaders. Leaders who are willing to break out of the old ways of doing things, and embracing much better and efficient ways of dealing with the business of life itself. This is where you come in. Leaders are not born, they are *made*. They are made by individuals surveying the terrain and rising to the occasion. You can do that your self. Why go through life doing things a certain way only because others have done it that way before you? Make your life better. Make your employees lives better. Make your company better. Make the world a better place for your children. Are these not worthy goals? And to top it all of, you have all the information available to you to do exactly that. And it is easier than anything you are doing right now. Change your thinking to a better way of doing business, and you will be happier and more prosperous than you ever thought possible. Do not follow old lines of thinking if they do not work to the best possible level. Always be on the lookout for better and more efficient ways of thinking. Your job as a leader is an extremely important job. Do your self and all those that depend on you a very big favor. Become the best leader that you possibly can. All the information is available to you. The payoff is incredibly good. You will do your self proud. No matter what I say, I can only hint at how good the payoff is. Play to *really* win. Be a real leader and the world is yours!

CHAPTER 6

▼

CRITICAL THINKING

Think of critical thinking as quality control for what you think. Since thinking is the basis for what you do, it is crucial that you make sure that your thinking works. The problem most managers make is that they fail to check out their thinking before they turn it into their way of doing things. That old train of thought that that is the way other managers do it, so it must work, just will not cut it. You have got to learn to check out everything that you do before you do it. If you just run with something before you check it out you will be taking a huge gamble. What happens if it doesn't work? And worse yet, what if it doesn't work and you don't know it? Every action that you build on false thinking is going to fail. Obviously, since you are reading this book you do not wish to fail any more or at the very least minimize any failures. You want to be a winner. That's good, because now we can have some fun. We are going to look at some standard lines of thought and check them out to see if they work or not. You are going to be surprised at some of the outcomes.

At every place that I have ever worked I always heard the managers talking about the same things. They always talked about improving teamwork, improving communication and improving morale. Every time they would say that "people are our most important resource", I would cringe. Because that was probably going to be the last thing that happened. The managers all knew what to say but they did not know how to do it. You have to be able to do more than talk the talk. You have to be able to make it happen. Since these managers were merely repeating what other managers did before them, they never learned how to do it right. They thought that just talking about it was good enough. It is not good enough. You absolutely have to make it happen. The mistake that they all made was they never stopped to think about the way they did things. If they had they would have realized that they were only talking about doing something and not doing it. By not using any critical thinking about their actions, they continued to build on a false line of thinking and everything they did after that would fail. They would *think* that they were good, but they could not back it up. You absolutely have to stop and check your thinking to make sure it works. Your motto should be simply "question everything". If you are not asking questions, you are not learning. Being a great manager is an ongoing job. You will never get to the end of it. You should always be asking questions and you should always be learning. Remember, you want to be the best manager on the planet. You will not get there by not asking questions.

Think of critical thinking as your own personal quality control laboratory. This is where you take lines of thinking and put them to the test before you use them. This is sort of where you test drive those lines of thinking. It is much better to test them out that to just jump in and start running with them. It will save you so much trouble. And why would the best manager on the planet want to deal with more trouble than is necessary? Besides, testing out those lines of thinking happens to be an awful lot of fun. Especially when you discover how much trouble some of these lines of thinking would cause you if you never questioned them at all. Here are a few of the things that I have looked into, and this is what I found.

LIFE ISN'T FAIR

Most all of us have said and or believed that old line that says "life isn't fair". I know I certainly have. But how many people have ever stopped to question that? So I did just that. Is that really true? Is life really unfair?

A while back a picture up to the newspaper of an old Vietnamese gentleman who had lost both of his arms and one of his legs in the war. He was in his early '60s and he was sitting in a marketplace somewhere in Vietnam selling his wares. What struck me about this picture were this gentleman's eyes. You would think that if anybody had a reason to be mad at life, it would have been this gentleman. But when you looked into his eyes, there was not a hint of sadness or anger in them. In fact, his eyes were brighter and more alive than most people I have ever met at any age. So, was life being unfair to this man and he was just too naive to understand that? He understood that it was not life that had done this to him. The war was started by a group of people, not life. He had made choices in his life that he was prepared to die for. He understood that people had started the war and not life itself. You could tell that from looking into his eyes. This man had an inner strength that radiated through his eyes. It would be easy for a lot of us to say that life had dealt this gentleman a bad hand indeed. A lot of people in this situation would have given up and felt sorry for themselves. I know I would have had an awful lot of trouble with his predicament, which is why I had so much respect for him. At one time he was my enemy.

Now at one time or another in your life and you have probably run across things that you do or thought were unfair. And sometimes, like me, you would even think that it was life itself that was being unfair to you. But here is a litmus test for you to apply to any given situation where you think unfairness occurs. I am not talking about whether the situation is fair or unfair, what I am talking about is the *source* of the unfairness. Is it life or something else entirely? If you feel unfairness has been dealt to you, trace the unfairness backwards until you find its source. Almost always you'll find the source of the unfairness to be a person or persons. You see, it is *people* that are unfair, not life. And if people are the source of the unfairness, then people can change that. Where do you go if you want to blame life for unfairness? It makes it very easy to be able to blame something that you cannot find. I have heard a lot of managers say "well, life just isn't fair". That is just plain wrong. Ninety nine point nine percent of the time it is people that are the source of the unfairness. Try it and see for yourself. So if we stop blaming life for unfairness and started seeking out the true source of the unfairness, we can begin to solve the problem. Blaming life for unfairness merely lets people off the hook. They do not have to take responsibility for their behavior if they can blame something that cannot be found. That it is not how a leader thinks. If he was the source of the unfairness then he fixes it and takes responsibility for it. If individuals would take responsibility for his or her behavior, the world would be a much better place. If you want to have some fun, the next time you hear someone say that life isn't fair, ask them to prove it. That will stop them in their tracks. Watch the blank look come over their faces.

How about something not so clear? A friend of mine had a 12-year-old son who had a brain tumor. There was no operation that could save him. He was going to die and there was nothing that could be done about it. This certainly seems like a true case of life being unfair. But is it? If there is something after we die and we do not know what it is, perhaps the answer is something that we do not know yet. There may be a reason for what appears to be a terrible tragedy to this family. So even though on the surface it does look like life being unfair, all the information is not in yet to make an informed decision. What happens after we die? We do not know yet that information. I cannot tell you either way whether life is being unfair or not. We will just have to wait and see. The possibility still exists that there may be a reason for it. Until then, we just have wait until all the information is in.

The easy way out sometimes is to blame someone else for our problems. If you do that for your entire life you will end up wasting your life. Life is a fantastic opportunity for each of us, and becomes even more so if we stop blaming each other and start to work together. That is how you go about reducing the unfairness that people put upon each other. If you blame others for your lot in life, even if it is warranted, you will still end up wasting your life. Is this a choice you wish to make?

I was reading the newspaper the other day, and there was a story about a baseball pitcher that tied the record for the most strikeouts in a 9 inning game. Unfortunately for him the game went into extra innings. So, tying the record did not count. The record was set up for a 9 inning game, not an extra inning game. Even though the pitcher had tied the record it would not count for him. The man that was in charge of the record-keeping for baseball, summed up in a single phrase. "Nobody said life was fair". Well, I'm saying it. I'm not just saying it, I am screaming it. Life is fair. It is people who are unfair. The sooner that we all understand that, the sooner we will really be able to solve our problems. As long as we continue to believe that life is not fair, we will never be able to find the source of our problems. And if you cannot find the source of the problem, you cannot solve it. Solving the problem gets rid of the problem.

Let's say that you were up for a promotion. There was you and another person up for the same job. Looking at the situation logically it appeared that you were the better choice of the two. However, the other person got the job. Maybe the other person was a favorite of the boss and you just got the short end of the stick. Life being unfair? Most likely the boss was making the call based on some line of thinking that just didn't work that well. Chances are that he was the one being unfair and did not notice it. Happens all the time. But, it is definitely not life that is being unfair. Unfortunately, it is usually poor judgment by *people* that is the root of most unfairness in this world.

THE TEAM BUILDERS

I once worked for a company that would send its managers off to different classes to improve the training of their managers. Now, lots of companies do that for their managers. Increasing your managers' ability to do their jobs better is a very good thing to do. However, there is something that you need to be on guard for when you do this. Remember, things aren't always what they appear to be on the surface.

What the corporate managers would do is to send their managers off to team building classes, for example. The managers would spend two or three days learning different techniques on team building. They would all work together as a team solving problems and learning the intricacies of running a team and what it was like to be part of a team. The classes they went to were very good. All the managers were taught some very important points on how to increase the team building that they could bring back to their teams. So, after all the classes were over the thinking was that they would come back to their teams with this new knowledge that they had learned, and incorporate into their teams and make them into much smoother and better running teams. The upper-level managers at corporate could pat themselves on their backs that they had sent their managers off to classes to become better managers. They had definitely held up their end of the bargain.

Unfortunately, that is not what actually occurred after they came back. The real problem was that the managers were already getting a payoff for doing their job the way it had always done before. So the problem became, why would the managers become better at their job? What was in it for them? They were already getting a payoff for doing the job the way they were doing it, so why would want to do more work? Now the upper-level managers would go on their way thinking all was well and that they had improved their company just a little bit better. But, do you know what actually occurred? The upper-level managers thought that things were better. However, the reality of the situation was the managers didn't change in all. They've brought nothing of what they had learned back into the team environment. They had no reason to. They were already getting a very nice payoff for doing the job the way they had always done before. There was no incentive for them. So in reality, after the managers came back from the classes, the status quo remained intact. Nothing had actually happened. However, upper level management actually *thought* something that occurred. What they should have done was to go back a short time later and check to see if the classes actually had any effect on the working environment. Had they had the good communication skills that we had talked about earlier in this book, they could have easily found the information that they needed. If they had bothered to come back and check, they would have found that nothing had changed. Then they could have changed their tactics and made sure that when they sent their managers to class, that the information their managers learned, would get transferred into the work environment, therefore accomplishing everything that upper-level management wanted to accomplish. So in reality they thought something occurred, when actually it had *not* occurred at all. Since they had not stopped to check to see if their line of thinking was working, they continued to build on a false line of thinking. So the question that has to come next is if they are making those mistakes in that arena, then what other arenas are they making mistakes? That is why you must constantly be checking out your thinking so that you do not end up away from your original intent. A simple visit to their plant later on would have shown them what was actually occurring. Problem solved. Now they will go on to make more mistakes and never even know it. Is that how you would choose to do it?

MERIT PAY

Merit pay is something that is used by companies to reward people who have done a better job than others. It's being talked about as a way to reward teachers who do a better job than others. It sounds great on the surface. But does it really work? Let's take a look.

The basic line of thinking behind merit pay is that you reward people who do a better job than others. Sounds fair to me. The first problem that we run into it is who decides who's doing a better job. Let's say that you are a manager of a group of people and you are to reward people based on their performance. Since there are all kinds of different managers in the world, each different type will have a different perspective on what a good job is. Some managers may like attendance and dependability, while other managers may like the fact that you do not make waves. So if you are manager of this group and you reward them based on your perspective of how they do their job, and then for some reason you are move to another job and another manager shows up, all of a sudden the rules for rewarding your people have not changed. The new manager may like to reward people for completely different aspects of their job. Now you have put your team in a position where they must continually adapt to each new manager. The one rewarded onetime may not be rewarded the next. If all managers see things exactly the same way, you would be able to reward your employees the same every time. But that is not reality. This is not a perfect world. So you can see that we're beginning to run into some serious problems here.

Let's look at something else. Let's say a team member is up for 50 cents an hour raise. And for some reason the manager does not think he deserves it. So the employee ends up with a zero raise. Maybe the employee got on the bad side of the manager or maybe he was having personal problems that didn't allow him to function at his best. Since most working years are calculated at 2020 hours a year, you can see that the raise amounts to approximately $1000 for the year. Usually by not giving an employee a raise you are trying to motivate them to do a better job. So does this motivate an employee? Next year, if the employee does an outstanding job, does he get his performance raise plus the money lost out on last year? Now let's say that that employee continues to work for your company for 20 years. Since the manager did not give that person a raise for that one year what really happens is that over 20 years the employee will basically be fined $20,000 in lost wages. Does this seem fair to you? (Don't be blaming life here.)

Now a lot of managers would think that by not giving that employee a raise for that one year was the end of it. But in reality, you can see that there is much more to it. Do you realize what kind of trouble you would have to get into to be fined $20,000 in court? And yet by denying that employee a 50 cent raise you have done just that. In real life merit pay is an extremely poor motivator of people. It looks good on the surface but fails when you think of it for more than a minute or two. All I have ever seen merit pay do is just piss people off. What usually ends up happening are major cases of favoritism. You cannot even accept the mere notion that favoritism may be occurring in your workplace.

It is much smarter to run a tight team that has communication, respect and leadership, and rewards that team as a team rather than to reward the individuals. There are just too many problems with rewarding individuals for it to be a viable option for you. You can still do that, but you take great risks and there is little payoff. Hopefully, the next time merit pay is mentioned you will not pay any attention.

SELF-CENTERED PEOPLE

I bring up the subject of self-centered people for reason. And like everything else in this book, the reason is simple. There is no such thing as a self-centered person. We have all known people that seem to think only of themselves. Whatever they did or whatever they said was really intended for the betterment of themselves. We have all been around people like that in our lives. They were always the people that you could not trust with any kind of information. Their whole world seemed only to revolve around themselves. But, I am telling you that there is no such thing as a self-centered person.

What is a self-centered person? We think of a person like that as someone who only cares about themselves. Everything that they do is done really to enhance their own position. I am sure that you have been around managers like that during your working life. They are the managers that are looking to move up the corporate ladder anyway that they can. So the characteristics of a self centered person are deceitfulness, lying, untrustworthiness and a general thinking that they are the center of the universe among other things. Now, the question that I have for you is, does this sound like a person that only cares about themselves? If I really cared about myself, would I do any of those negative things that a self-serving person would do? How can I say that I cared about myself and yet did so many negative things around other people? If I really cared about myself and my own betterment, I would do none of the above. You see, the fact is that that person does not care about themselves at all. If I would give them a name, I would call them callous and indifferent. A callous and indifferent person being a person who cares about little or nothing at all. That is a much better fit for a description of that person. They do not care about you and they do not care about themselves. If they did, they would not act like that at all. Those kinds of people are not only dangerous to you, but also dangerous to themselves. They are doing nothing that enhances who they are. They are merely destructors. When you run into these people and you will, smile and tell them what ever they want to hear. Do not ever tell them anything more.

Avoid them at all costs, if you can. They do not bring out the best in anyone. Not even themselves.

You cannot do negative things with your life and care about yourself at the same time. It is just not possible. If you care about yourself, you will do things that enhance your position as a human being on this planet. You will do just the opposite of what a so-called self centered person would do. You cannot care about yourself and destroy yourself at the same time.

DIFFERENT MANAGERS

Along the same lines is the fact that there are different kinds of managers. I'm sure by now on that you have seen many different kinds of management styles. I was reading a book the other day about how to impress your boss by understanding all the different styles of management. His words did have some merit, because that is how the actual work environment is. But is that the best? The problem with all the different styles of management is that your employees must continually adapt to each new style. That in itself is the very thing that destroys merit pay. If I am the CEO of a corporation, I want my managers to basically think all along the same lines. Like attracts like. But this time in a positive direction. Why do I want my employees to spend an inordinate amount of time adapting to each new manager? I am not saying that you cannot be different. What I am saying it is that each manager must have the same kind of foundation, then those managers can bring to the table their own styles. That way you end up with the best of both worlds. You end up with a fairly standard way of managing your people that is tried and true and you get the individuality that brings creativity to the table. That is a win-win situation. Besides, the author of that book was a believer in the old adage that "life isn't fair". That in itself made me wonder about what he was saying in the rest of his book. He just didn't ask enough questions.

ASK QUESTIONS

Think for your self! If you let other people do your thinking for you, you end up living their life, not yours. Is this a conscious choice that you wish to make? By doing a little bit of questioning about accepted or suggested ways of doing things, you can save yourself, your employees and your company a lot of time and trouble by not doing unnecessary things. Critical thinking on your part is essential to being a leader. You must always be looking at everything to make sure that it will actually work in your environment. Go past that one minute surface look at ideas and check them out to see what is really going on underneath. It is just a smart way to go. The best managers on the planet do not waste their time on ideas that either do not work or bring dysfunction into the team. So many managers that I have been around made most of their mistakes because they did not do a little bit of critical thinking. Do you wish to waste all or most of your working life doing things that function poorly. *This is your one and only life.* You must pay attention to save yourself, your employees and your company a lot of grief.

CHAPTER 7

▼

PASSION

Passion is the engine that drives your work. Without passion your work is lifeless. You merely go through the motions of your job without any enthusiasm. You are unable to inspire anyone around you, let alone yourself. Remember, you are a leader. If you want your people to be inspired and passionate about their work, you must lead them to that inspiration and passion. You can be that leader that brings out the passion for living and for working that your people need. They are just waiting for you to come along. Remember, they expect you to fail, not to succeed. You actually have a captive audience, so it is all up to you. So why would you want to go on doing an ordinary job, facing all the same problems over and over again on a daily basis, when you can change all that. Every problem that you encounter can be overcome and gotten rid of so that you do not have to deal with the same problems day after day after day. By having a passion for what you do, you are able to overcome obstacles that no manager with an ordinary outlook can overcome. To do the job the way an ordinary manager does, is a highly inefficient way of doing things and shows that they are not paying attention. Is this any way to live your life? Remember, this is your one and only life. It is up to you to make the most of it. There is no reason that you have to continue doing things the way they have always been done with all the inherent problems, when you can change all of that, and you can do so much better in your life and also with the lives of the people that you manage. It is simply a no-brainer choice. And all you have to do are some simple little things. And if you are doing any of the things in this book, then you are already doing some of the simple little things.

When you bring your passion for leadership to your work, you bring out more passion in your employees. And by doing so you are starting to bring out the best in yourself and your employees and raising their comfort level. Remember comfort level? That is a key to measuring your success as a manager. Most people have never had a great leader in the life, but were stuck with some dull ordinary manager and they were living out a dull and ordinary life. Just going through the motions of life, like so many people do. And then a passionate leader comes along and inspires them to do better with their life and their work. What if that leader is you? Well it can be you. Are you prepared to tell me or better yet yourself, that that is not something that is worthy of pumping your fist for? And you thought that only people like Tiger Woods were able to do that.

When you go to work tomorrow put a smile on your face. Walk around and talk to each of your employees and asked them how they are doing. Bring in some doughnuts. When was the last time that you told your employees how glad you were that they were working for you? When was the last time you told them that you were proud to come to work every day and work side-by-side with them? Asked them about their kids. Asked them about the wife, if they are married. Asked them if they need any help that day. Give them an extra break just for the heck of it. Step in and do their job and let them take 10 or 15 minutes off just for the fun of it. And by the way, whatever happened to fun? When did work stop being fun? When did work become a four letter word? It is not going to be all fun, but you can certainly have more fun at work in if you give it a little bit of a try. It is up to you to set the stage. If you want your people to have more fun and be happier then you do it first. All you have to think about is how much better work will be if you just do a few of these things. They will cost little or nothing to do, but bring you great rewards. Again, why would you want to do it any other way?

It is all about passion. Just rev up the engines and go get it. This is another one of those things that just keeps getting easier every day you do it. Sure there are going to be bad days. Big deal. Just get back up the next day and start it back up. One of the traits about human beings is that we adapt to our environment. If you make passion a daily commitment, pretty soon you and your employees will adapt to a passionate environment. It will become second nature to the whole team. Think for a minute about coming to work on any given day and finding a passionate and tight running team waiting for you. Think about how much different that would be than going in to work tomorrow is going to be.

I once watched a manager giving a speech to his employees. He wanted his employees to act like the men who work at the Pike Place fish market in Seattle. They are the guys that throw the fish to each other as the customers are buying them. Now when they do their job it looks like these men are having one heck of a good time doing their job. They are very upbeat people with a good deal of teamwork and a very happy attitude about their job. Now this manager was telling his employees that that was the example they should shoot for while they were doing their job. He wanted his employees to emulate the men that worked at that fish market. So, guess what happened? That's right, nothing. This manager thought that all he had to do was to tell his people how he wanted them to do their job. He never realized that if he wanted his employees to act like that, he had to act like that himself. It would certainly make it really nice if all you had to do was to ask your people to have higher morale and better teamwork and better communication. But it doesn't work that way. If you want your employees to have passion about their job, you have to have passion about your job. That is the only way it works. Besides, if all you had to do was ask, what would you learn? What would your employees learn? You have to do the work if you want the reward. And like I have been telling you all along, the work is easy. So ask yourself why you would want to do it with any other way?

Passion extends to other areas as well. Do you know what customer service really is? It is the measure of a company's humanity. That is to say, how much your company really cares about people. The companies that have the best customer service are always the companies that care the most about their customers as *people,* not just customers. There are a lot of people out there that think that business is simply business. That is not true at all. Business is about people. If there are no people, then there is no business. The more that you care about people and the satisfaction that they have with your product or service, the more successful your company is going to be. The companies that you read about that have problems are usually companies that care the least about their customers. They may talk about taking care about their customers, but the bottom line is they care less about them than they say. It is easy to talk about something. It is awful easy to think you are good. The bottom line always is your track record with your customers. Be able to back it up with your customers. Inside of your company or out.

Customer service extends not only to your customers, but also to the people that work in your company as well. How you treat your employees is also a measure of your customer service. How well two groups interact in a company is a measure of those groups customer service towards each other. Customer service is everywhere within your company. The best companies always understand this. It is something that is very easy to do. If as a manager you see your employees and your customers as one in the same, you will be far ahead of your peer group. Winning is simply paying attention, gathering information and then doing the job. This is another place where your passion comes in. The more passionate that you are about your people, the more successful you are going to be in business. You must listen to your customers, whether they are customers outside your company or customers within your company. The more information that you can gather and then act upon, the more successful you are going to be. It is really very simple. Where people get into trouble is, they let their ego into the game and/or they use lines of thinking that do not work. Just about every business that does poorly makes those two mistakes. Just don't do them. Care about yourself, care about your people, care about your customers, be able to back it up, and you will be a very, very successful manager.

CHAPTER 8

▼

PUTTING IT ALL TOGETHER

Now that you know the 6 things that it takes to be the best manager on the planet and you have made a reality check of your ideas, you are ready to put it all together. All this book has been about are the things it takes into make you a winner. If you have gotten this far and you have not thrown the book out the window, then I can presume that you are interested in being the best manager on this planet, or at the very least a better manager. Everything that I have talked about is simple and easy to do, but there's a catch to it. You just have to do it. Do not be fooled by how easy it may seem. Some people think that the harder they work, the more they must be getting done. That is not always true. And it is definitely not true with management. There are going to be times when you may have to make some tough decisions. That just comes with the territory. But by doing the things I have talked about you are going to be in the best shape that you can to make those decisions. They would be much harder if you did it any other way. And I can tell you from experience that when it comes time to make those decisions, you will not want them to be any harder.

Every one of us has been given the best computer on this planet, free of charge, right between our ears. Your brain can do more than any supercomputer on this planet. You have the ability to think. Use that ability to your best advantage. I will be the first to admit that there are some hard drives out there that seem to be a little sluggish, if not down right small. Some people seem to think that their brain is nothing more than a cranial airbag to keep their skull from imploding. Unfortunately, there are just some things that we have to live with.

Everything that you have read about in this book will help you to become a better manager. I realize that you are not going to agree with everything that I have said. That's okay. Perhaps at the very least it will serve as the stimulus for your own version. But that is the fun and the beauty of doing your job as a manager. Like I said, it is the most important job on this planet right now. It does not matter whether you are the President of the United States or you are in charge of the gas station down on the corner. It is all the same playing field. Your job as a manager is just as important as anyone else's job as a manager. It is a wide-open field simply because most managers do not pay attention to how to do their job properly. They follow in the same old ruts of thinking that others before them have done. They asked little, if any questions. They challenge little or nothing. I am happy to say that you do not have to follow in their footsteps. You can have as much fun as you like. There really is no limit. The only limits that exist are the limits that people apply to themselves. You do not have to be one of those people. You realize now that you only have one life and it is important that you live it well. From now on you get to change the world for the better. If that is not exciting, then what it is?

Hopefully, you are beginning to see your job as a manager in a different light. You can see possibilities that did not seem to exist before. You see your job not as a watcher of people, but as a leader of people. You know the difference between sitting on the sidelines and actively engaging your people and your job. You see all that is taken for granted at work is something that can be change for the better. The problems that most people think are so inherent in any job situation are not inherent in the way you see the job now. You know that work does not have to be a four letter word. You understand just how many people you really affect on any given day that you go to work. In short, you see things as they could be not how they are. That is a very impressive accomplishment in and of itself. You are now becoming one of the few instead of one of the many. Being a very good manager is a lot like common sense. It just isn't that common.

To be a good manager of people is a very worthwhile profession. It is not a matter of money and status. It is far more than that. You can now begin to see that there's far more to your job than you first realized. You have seen beneath the surface of your job. You see the possibilities. What appeared tired now appears new and fresh. A simple change in your point of view and all becomes better.

You do not have to do everything that is in this book. In fact, I encourage you to try just a little bit of it. Take something simple and give it a test run. Kick the tires. Take it for a test drive. Use your critical thinking on what I have said to you. Go to work tomorrow and have some fun. That is a great way to start it off. Get any pressure off yourself right away. Having fun is actually the easiest way to get started. Take whatever you feel comfortable with and try that first.

You are now at the turning point in your life as a manager. This is your opportunity to change your life and the lives of the people around you. You are a leader now…not just someone who is merely a manager in name only. All that is possible as a leader sits before you. You are the one who now controls your future.

I'll be the first to tell you that not everything will go smoothly. There are going to be people that you run into who do not wish to be awakened from their slumber. These are the people that I call the "sleepwalkers". They wish to stay asleep their whole lives if possible. They wish only to sleepwalk through life without ever stepping up to enjoy life to its fullest. They only want the illusion of success without ever having to actually accomplish it. They believe in what they do. But they all have a singular problem. They can not back it up. There is a certain sadness about these people. However you know now that there's more to life and your job than has been shown to you before. Hopefully you have begun to see that sleepwalking through life is actually a waste of life. You only have one life and you do not wish to waste it. Do not let these people derail you from what you wish to accomplish. After a while they will leave you alone because they sense an inner strength in you. They will know that you are focused on a place that they do not wish to go. Do not worry though, because you have made the right choice.

By doing things that I have told you about in this book you are going to change your life for the better. I have said it before in this book and I will say it again. Everything about your job, your life and your people will be better because of what you have chosen to do from now on. You will notice a feeling inside of you that is born of your confidence. You are going to walk taller and straighter than you ever have before. You are going to be proud of yourself, your people and what you have all accomplished together. You're on the verge of something very, very exciting in your life. And after doing this for a while, you're going to notice that other people treat you differently. They will sense that confidence and self-assuredness that you are going to have. They are going to sense that they are dealing with someone that has a special-purpose in this life. It is going to be something that other people will pick up on. And you will notice that in them. It will be because you have chosen to step out onto a path of serious personal power. Your life and the lives of the people around you are going to change for the better.

You are being presented with a very special opportunity. That is because the information in this book is tried, true and rock solid. It will make you into a great manager. If nothing else, it will make you into a very good manager. We definitely need all the good managers that we can get. What you do as a manager is very important. It is a very noble occupation. When the time is right in your life, you'll try a little bit of this. You will be pleased with the results. Remember, this is your one and only life. Do not to waste it.

www.ingramcontent.com/pod-product-compliance
Lightning Source LLC
Chambersburg PA
CBHW030851180526
45163CB00004B/1525